I dedicate this book to my twin brother David,
who loves cooking and food as much as I do!

Published in 2010 by:
The Irish Farmers Journal
Irish Farm Centre, Bluebell, Dunlin 12
01-4199500 | www.farmersjournal.ie

© Irish Farmers Journal / Neven Maguire 2010
©Photographs: Irish Farmers Journal 2010

ISBN: 9780953490226

Irish Farmers Journal & Irish Country Living: Mairead Lavery, David Leydon,
Penny Osborne, Jack Caffrey, Owen McGauley

Design: Márla.ie, Waterford
Editing: Orla Broderick
Print: Johnswood Press, Dublin
Photography: Jack Caffrey, Irish Farmers Journal
Food Stylist: Sharon Aherne-Smith

Rebuilding Lives Affected By Childhood Cancer

BARRETSTOWN

a Hole in the Wall Camp.

"At Barretstown, a magical castle in the foothills of the Wicklow
Mountains in Ireland, children with cancer and other serious
illnesses come for some serious fun. The children and their families
take part in a unique programme of Therapeutic Recreation
recognized by the medical world as playing an important part in
their recovery from serious illness. Thank you for your support."

Foreword from Neven Maguire

Over the past two years, I have enjoyed a long and truly fulfilling relationship with the Farmers Journal and its readers; perhaps this is because we share a similar passion for using only the finest, local produce. Through my work with the team at the Farmers Journal, I have had the pleasure of meeting food producers from all regions of the country, and have enjoyed that immensely.

Compiling this book, Neven's Country Living in conjunction with the Farmers Journal has been a great project; so many readers have asked us to do this since I first started writing for the Journal, we thought it was time to honour their requests! You generally seem to want the same things when it comes to recipes: good, delicious, nutritious meals that are easy to prepare and guaranteed to have everyone coming back for seconds.

I've certainly kept this in mind when coming up with the final selection of recipes – after all, cooking for our families is the most important thing in our lives, so when it comes to mealtimes we want to give them the best we can. For me there is nothing better than cooking and eating really good home-cooked food with people I really care about.

The book is divided into sections that reflect the whole range of occasions you might want to cater for such as: Breakfasts and Brunch with lots of yummy dishes to start off the day; Starters and Soups, full of delicious ideas for appetizers and a wide variety of soups to suit every occasion; Lamb, Beef and Game filled with plenty of heart warming casseroles; Chicken and Pork packed with lots of effortless meals; Vegetarian, whether you are catering for an individual in the family or just want a meat-free meal there's a recipe here for you; Family Favourites, plenty of quick, tasty and satisfying meals that everyone will enjoy; Fish and Seafood, great recipes that are easy to prepare; Desserts so that you can conjure up fabulous treats; Baking in the Afternoon, to ensure that the tradition of passing on your cookery skills is never forgotten; and the Ultimate Christmas which has every recipe you'll need to ensure the festive holiday is a perfect meal that is completely stress-free.

You can of course mix and match the dishes, but I hope that whatever the occasion, you'll find a recipe that fits the bill. Please feel free to experiment with your own variations on the recipes because cooking should be lots of fun. Remember, support your local producers and retailers when shopping for your ingredients and always look out for the Bord Bia Quality Assured Mark. So now it just remains for me to say that I hope you thoroughly enjoy using Neven's Country Living, I hope this book brings you years of enjoyable cooking, and lots of happy memories to cherish.

Neven Maguire
Chef & Proprietor
Macnean House & Restaurant

Foreword from Farmers Journal

Neven Maguire's passion for cooking is contagious and his down to earth approach appeals to people of all ages. The first time I met Neven, he was surrounded by a group of teenagers and he had them enthralled talking about his work as a chef. But he was also listening intently and it was plain to see he was genuinely interested in their views. Only later did I discover that he backs up that interest by offering many youngsters work experience at McNean's, his renowned restaurant at Blacklion, County Cavan.

Another group of people Neven is enthusiastic about are our food producers. He has forged solid relationships with farmers and proudly displays the names of all his suppliers in his restaurant. He is acknowledged as a great ambassador of Irish food both at home and abroad.

So it was a perfect partnership when Neven became Food Writer with Irish Country Living two years ago. This magazine is part of the Irish Farmers Journal and when it comes to food our aim is to showcase the best of Irish produce, always making the link between farm and fork.

This ethos which is important to us is shared by Neven Maguire and that's what makes him so popular with our readers. They love his food pages and we know many of them cut out and file his recipes for future reference. Over and over again they have asked us to gather these recipes, which are unique to Irish Country Living, into a cookery book. And that's exactly what we have done.

It's always a pleasure to work with Neven and it was especially so when compiling this lovely cookery book. With over 100 favourite recipes I'm sure it will become a mainstay in many kitchens where good food is prepared, eaten and appreciated.

Mairead Lavery
Editor, Irish Country Living

Irish Country Living, Ireland's favourite country magazine, is free with the Irish Farmers Journal every Thursday.

CONTENTS

BREAKFAST AND BRUNCH

HEALTHY MUESLI WITH SUMMER BERRIES

Muesli is really easy to make up, and you can keep it in an airtight container, adding different fruits. Sliced bananas, strawberries, raspberries, or blueberries are all great. I like to serve it with a good quality organic natural yoghurt. To make this into a fruit granola, drizzle the porridge oats with two tablespoons each of sunflower oil and brown sugar or maple syrup before baking.

INGREDIENTS

MAKES 725G (1LB 6OZ)

500g (1lb 2oz) porridge oats

125g (4 ½oz) dried fruits, chopping up any larger pieces (such as sultanas, apricots, cranberries, dates)

50g (2oz) mixed seeds (such as linseeds, pumpkin seeds, sunflower seeds)

50g (2oz) mixed nuts, roughly chopped (such as hazelnuts, almonds, pecans)

yoghurt, summer berries (such as raspberries, strawberries, blueberries, blackberries) and clear honey (optional), to serve

METHOD

To make the muesli, simply toss the oats, dried fruits, seeds and nuts together in a large bowl. This will keep in an airtight container for as long as the best-by dates on the packs.

Pour out the desired portion of muesli into a serving bowl. Spoon on your favourite yoghurt (natural works particularly well with this). To serve, top with a mix of summer berries and a drizzle of honey if desired.

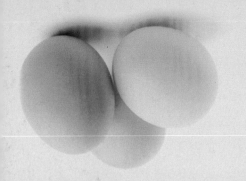

SCRAMBLED EGGS WITH IRISH HOT SMOKED SALMON

Another favourite of mine is scrambled egg with hot smoked salmon. If you prefer your scrambled eggs more chunky, do not whisk the egg and milk mixture – pour or break the eggs straight into the pan and then add the cream, stirring continuously. I much prefer to fold in the hot smoked salmon at the very end of cooking, to keep its texture.

INGREDIENTS

SERVES 4

6 eggs
3 tbsp milk
1 tbsp snipped fresh chives
40g (1½oz) butter
175g (6oz) hot smoked salmon, skinned and flaked
4 slices multi-grain bread
salt and freshly ground black pepper
fresh long chives, to garnish (optional)

METHOD

Preheat the grill. Whisk together the eggs, milk, chives and plenty of freshly ground black pepper. Heat a knob of the butter in a non-stick frying pan until foaming. Add the egg mixture and whisk continuously for 2–3 minutes, until just set but still soft. Remove from the heat, as they will continue to cook, and gently fold in the hot smoked salmon. Check the seasoning and add a pinch of salt if you think it needs it.

Meanwhile, toast the bread on a grill rack, then spread each piece of toast with the remaining butter and cut into triangles. Arrange two of the toasted bread triangles on each warmed plate and top each one with the scrambled eggs with hot smoked salmon. Garnish with the chives, if liked, to serve.

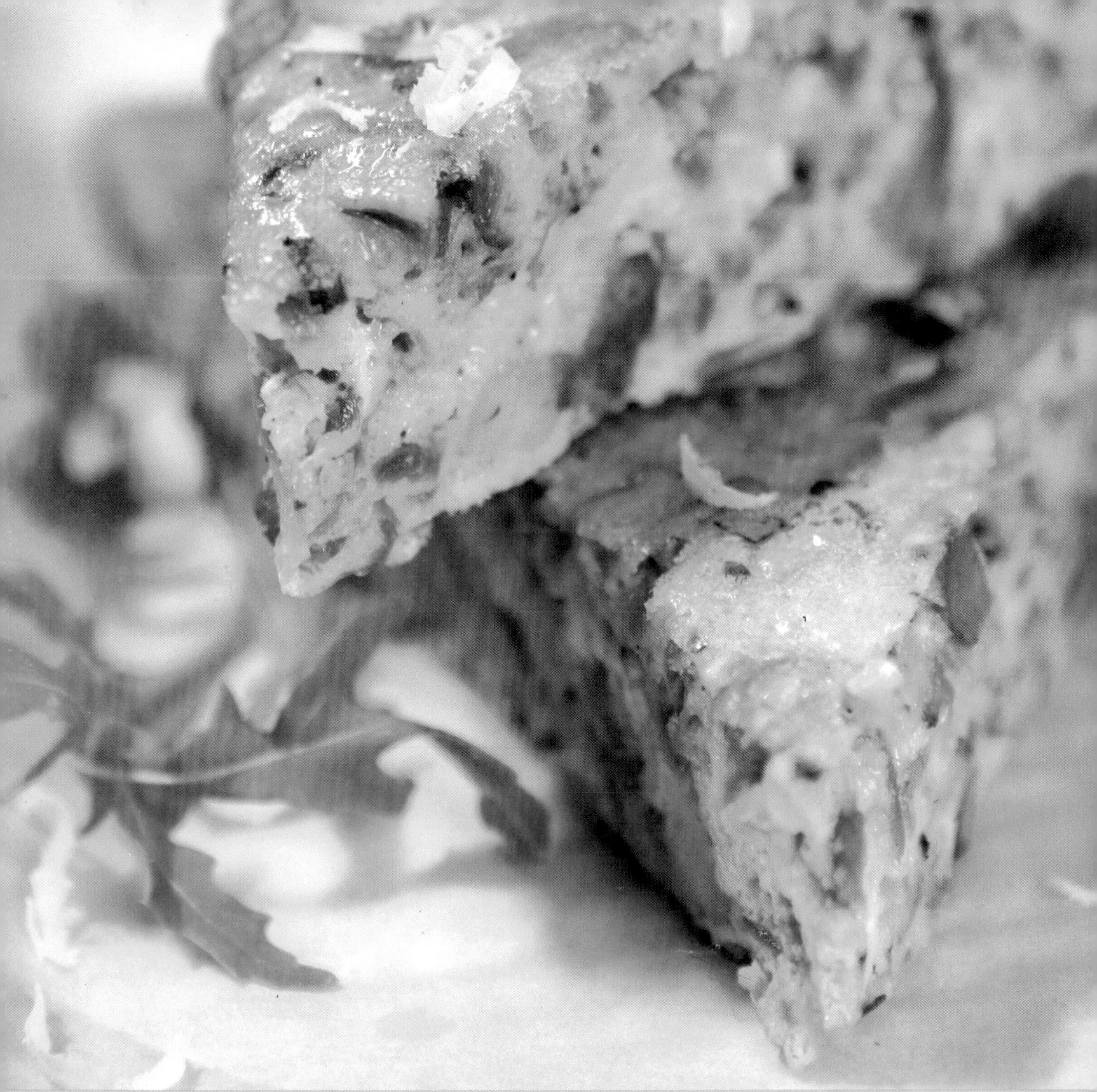

SMOKED BACON FRITTATA WITH PARMESAN CHEESE

Don't be tempted to over beat the eggs as it will spoil the texture. A combination of wild mushrooms sautéed in butter and served on the side — such as shitake, oyster and chantrelle — that most supermarkets are now stocking, would make this into a very special breakfast indeed.

INGREDIENTS

SERVES 4

2 tbsp olive oil
25g (1oz) butter
3 Spanish onions, thinly sliced
6 rindless smoked bacon rashers, cut into small lardons
1 tsp fresh thyme leaves
3 garlic cloves, crushed
8 large eggs, lightly beaten
50g (2oz) freshly grated Parmesan
1 tsp finely chopped fresh sage
salt and freshly ground black pepper
Wild rocket to garnish

METHOD

Heat one tablespoon of the oil and the butter in a large sauté or frying pan. Add the onions and start by cooking over a fairly high heat, stirring constantly until they begin to soften but not brown. Then reduce the heat and continue to cook over a medium heat, stirring frequently so the onions do not stick or brown. They will need about 30 minutes in total to caramelise.

Stir the bacon into the onion mixture with the thyme and garlic 5 minutes before the end of cooking time and continue to cook until the bacon has begun to sizzle and crisp up. Tip into a large bowl and leave to cool for at least 5 minutes. Season generously.

Preheat the oven to 180°C (350°F), Gas mark 4. Add the eggs, Parmesan and sage to the onions and stir well to combine. You should have 1.2 litres (2 pints) of mixture in total. Heat the remaining oil in an ovenproof heavy-based pan, that is about 23cm (9in), in diameter and deep enough to take the mixture. Swirl to coat the sides of the pan evenly, then pour in the egg mixture and cook for 6–8 minutes over a low heat to set the bottom and sides. Transfer the pan to the oven and cook, uncovered, for about 20 minutes until just set, puffed up and lightly golden. Loosen the sides with a palette knife and cut the frittata into wedges and serve warm or cold on to plates. Garnish with rocket to serve.

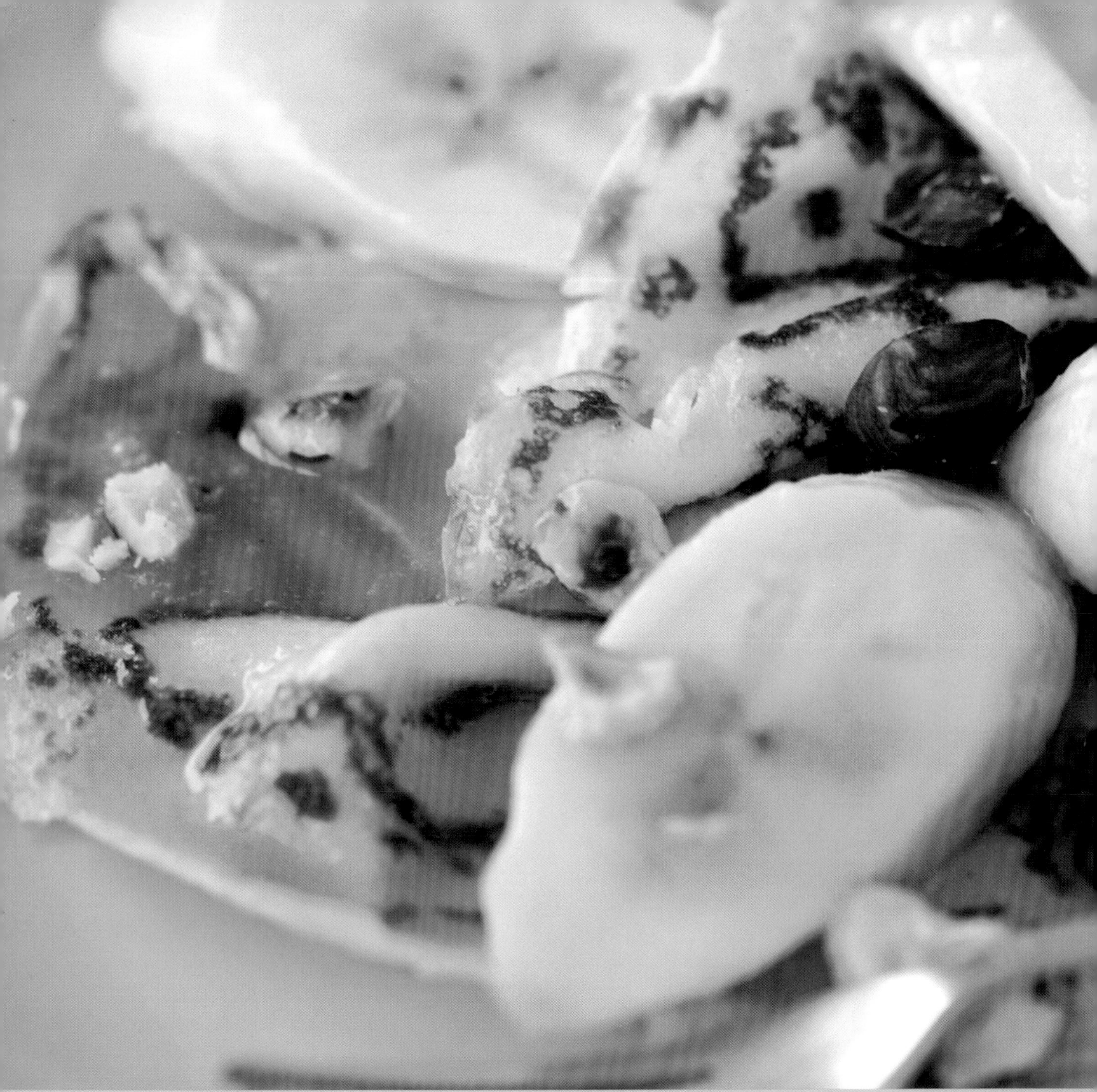

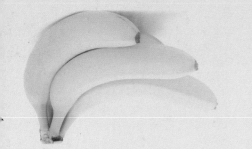

BANANA AND BUTTERSCOTCH PANCAKES

If you want to make these pancakes before serving them up, stack them with a square of greaseproof paper between each one. They will sit happily like this for a couple of hours. The batter benefits from resting for at least half an hour but would be fine for a couple of days in the fridge if it is covered with clingfilm. While the butterscotch sauce will keep for two weeks in the fridge.

INGREDIENTS

SERVES 4

100g (4oz) plain flour
pinch of salt
1 egg
300ml (½ pint) milk
25g (1oz) butter, melted
sunflower oil, for cooking
3 bananas
1 lemon, halved and pips removed
50g (2oz) toasted hazelnuts (optional)

FOR THE BUTTERSCOTCH SAUCE:

150g (5oz) caster sugar
120ml (4fl oz) cream
40g (1 ½oz) butter
¼ vanilla pod, seeds only
crème fraîche, to serve

METHOD

To make the butterscotch sauce, place the sugar in a heavy-based saucepan with 150ml (¼ pint) of water. Bring to the boil and cook for approximately 15 minutes, until golden brown. Stir in the cream, butter and vanilla seeds and mix well to combine. Stir over a low heat to a thick consistency and keep warm.

Sift the flour and salt together. Beat the egg into the milk and whisk into the flour. Add the melted butter. Let it rest for 30 minutes. Warm the pancake pan and add enough oil to cover the base. Tip some batter into the pan and tilt the pan so that the mixture covers the base in a thin layer. Cook for 15-20 seconds, until golden brown. Flip over and cook the other side. Keep warm.

Peel the bananas and then cut into thick slices. Sprinkle with lemon juice. Put a pancake on a plate and drizzle over some butterscotch sauce. Arrange the bananas on top, drizzle some more butterscotch sauce over it and sprinkle with some toasted nuts, if desired. Fold the pancake in half. Serve with a dollop of crème fraîche.

BLACKLION PORRIDGE WITH IRISH MIST HONEY AND CREAM

Porridge is one of our most popular breakfasts in the restaurant, and this recipe goes down a treat. On cold winter mornings, it gets you off to a good start and takes no more than 10 minutes to prepare.

INGREDIENTS

SERVES 4

100g (4oz) porridge oats (organic if possible)

300ml (½ pint) whole-fat milk (plus a little extra if necessary)

4 dsp clear honey

4 dsp Irish mist

150ml (¼ pint) cream (optional)

METHOD

Simmer the porridge oats and milk together in a saucepan for 8–10 minutes, until the mixture is slightly thickened, stirring all the time. It is important that the porridge has a nice soft dropping consistency so add a little more milk if you think that it needs it.

To serve, spoon the porridge into warmed bowls. Drizzle each one with some honey and Irish Mist and finally, serve with cream if you wish.

THE MACNEAN SPECIAL BREAKFAST

This is a simplified version of the full Irish that we serve to guests. Normally there's some boiled boxty with it and a slice of pan-fried pork liver. It's important to me that it leaves a marked impression as it is going to be the last thing customers have to eat before they leave. It has a number of different elements and is not actually as easy as it looks so needs a bit of clever timing if the results are going to be perfect. Obviously you could grill everything for a healthier option.

INGREDIENTS

SERVES 4

4-8 pork and leek sausages
sunflower oil, for frying
2 vine ripened tomatoes, halved
butter, for grilling and frying
4 slices each black and white pudding
4 rindless back bacon rashers (preferably dry cured)
4 potato bread farls
225g (8oz) flat mushrooms, sliced
4 eggs
salt and freshly ground black pepper

METHOD

Preheat the oven to 150°C (300°F), Gas mark 2 and preheat the grill. Fry the sausages in a little sunflower oil over a medium heat, turning every now and then, for 8-10 minutes until cooked through. Put on to a baking sheet and slide into the oven.

Arrange the tomatoes cut-side up on a grill rack, dot with a little butter and season to taste. Place the black and white pudding alongside and grill for 4-5 minutes, turning the puddings once, then put in the oven. Meanwhile, wipe out the frying pan, add a teaspoon or two of oil and fry the bacon for 1-2 minutes on each side until crisp and golden brown. Keep warm with the sausages, black and white puddings and tomatoes.

Heat another tablespoon of oil with the bacon fat left in the frying pan, add the potato bread farls and fry for 1-2 minutes on each side until crisp and golden. Put on to a second baking tray and slide into the oven.

Melt a small knob of butter in a medium frying pan, add the mushrooms and season to taste, then cook over a high heat for 2-3 minutes. Set to one side.

Wipe the frying pan clean again, heat a thin layer of oil in it over a medium-high and break in the eggs. Season to taste and fry for a couple of minutes, spooning a little of the hot fat over the yolks, until just set.

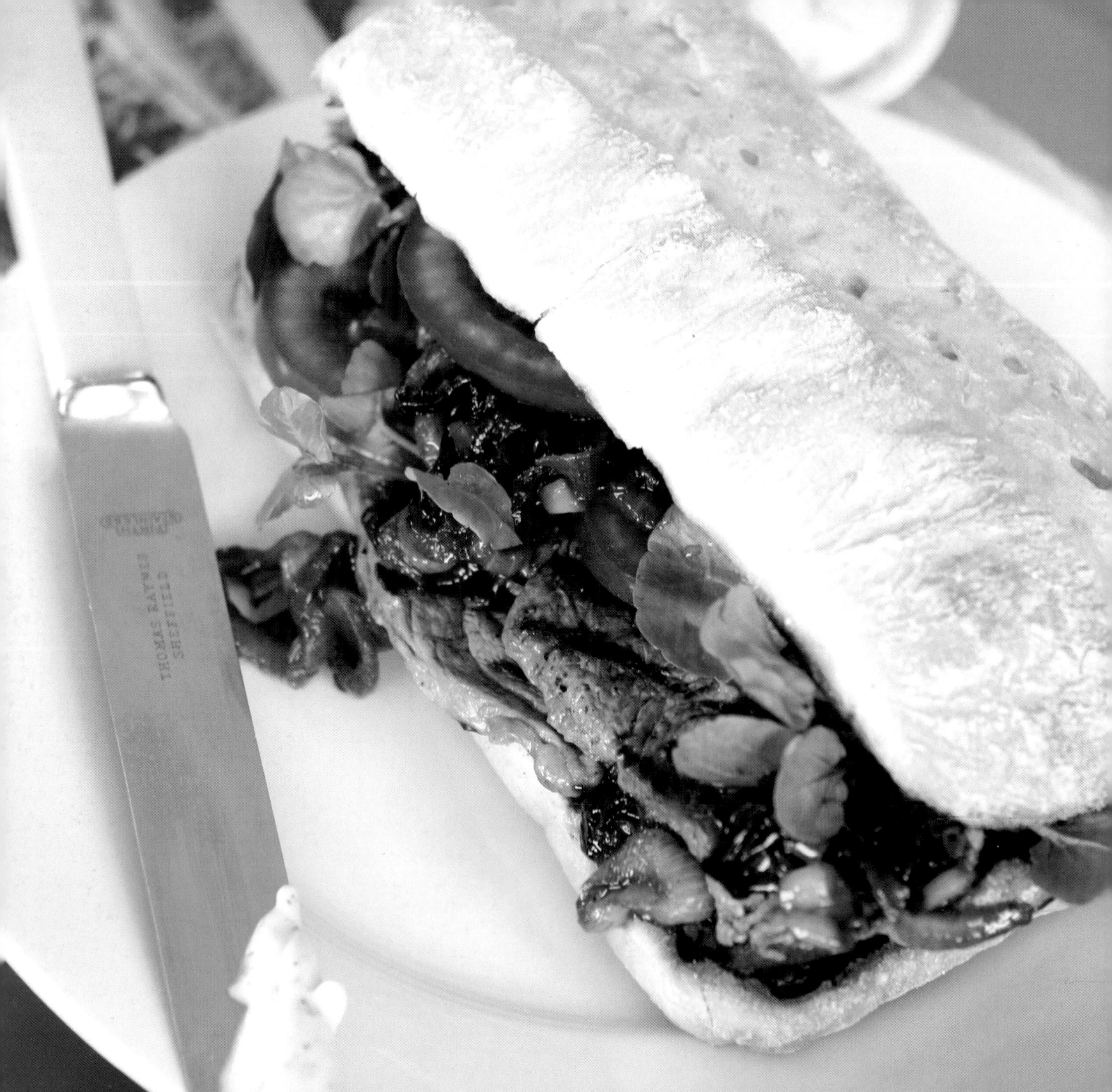
THOMAS RAYNES
SHEFFIELD

STEAK AND ONION SANDWICH

There are times at the weekend when you want something tasty and delicious but just don't feel like cooking a full meal. This is one of those dishes I find myself cooking again and again. If you want to make it even more substantial try serving it with crisp, fat chips and watch how quickly the plates are cleared!

INGREDIENTS

SERVES 4

2 tbsp olive oil
2 large red onions, cut into thin rings
1 tbsp soft brown sugar
2 ciabatta loaves, cut half half to open
4 x 175g (6oz) thin cut rump or
sirloin steak
8 tbsp mayonnaise
4 tsp wholegrain mustard
4 vine ripened tomatoes, sliced
50g (2oz) watercress, thick stalks removed
salt and freshly ground black pepper

METHOD

Heat one tablespoon of oil in a frying pan. Fry the onions over a low heat for about 10 minutes, stirring occasionally until golden and softened. Add the sugar and cook, stirring for a further 2 minutes until the sugar has dissolved and the onions become sticky. Keep warm.

Heat a griddle pan over a high heat and toast the ciabatta halves cut-side down for a few minutes, until charred. Drizzle the remaining tablespoon of oil over the steaks and season with salt and freshly ground black pepper. Griddle for 3 minutes each side or according to taste.

Meanwhile, mix the mayonnaise and mustard together in a small bowl. Layer the tomato slices, watercress and sticky onions onto the toasted ciabatta. Place the steak on top of each serving and spoon on the mustard mayonnaise. Serve immediately.

SMOKED BACON AND EGG CROISSANT WITH TOMATO RELISH

These filled croissants are always a winner at breakfast and are an excellent way of using up day old croissants. However they also freeze very well and I often keep some tucked away for those unplanned mornings after the night before …

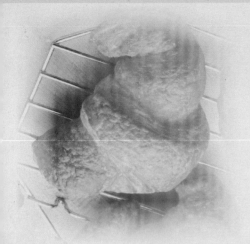

INGREDIENTS

SERVES 4

8 rindless smoked streaky bacon rashers

4 croissants

2 tbsp sunflower oil

4 eggs

FOR THE TOMATO RELISH:

2 vine ripened tomatoes, finely chopped

2 spring onions, finely chopped

1 tbsp balsamic vinegar

large pinch of caster sugar

2 fresh basil leaves, finely chopped

METHOD

To make the tomato relish, place the tomatoes, spring onions, vinegar, sugar and basil in a saucepan and cook for 10-15 minutes until the tomatoes have softened, stirring occasionally. Season to taste and leave to cool.

Preheat the grill and arrange the bacon on a grill rack, then cook for 5-6 minutes until crisp, turning once. Slice the croissants, then open out and place the slices of crispy bacon inside.

Heat a large frying pan and add the oil, swirling to coat the base evenly. Break in the eggs and cook for 2 minutes or longer, if you prefer your eggs less runny, gently spooning the excess oil over the yolks to help them cook. Using a fish slice, carefully lift the eggs into the croissants and top each one with a spoonful of the tomato relish. Serve immediately.

CRISPY BACON SALAD WITH BLACK PUDDING AND POACHED EGG

This is a perfect recipe for a weekend brunch and once you've mastered how to poach the eggs, the rest is a doodle. I normally make mine in advance so that I just have to reheat them as needed. To do this simply gently lower them into a pan of simmering water for 30 seconds or so.

INGREDIENTS
SERVES 4

4 eggs
2 tbsp white wine vinegar
4 tbsp extra-virgin olive oil
175g (6oz) black pudding, skinned and cut into 1cm (½in) slices
4 rindless bacon rashers
175g (6oz) mixed baby salad leaves
1 tsp wholegrain mustard
½ tsp clear honey
salt and freshly ground black pepper
crusty bread, to serve

METHOD

To make the poached eggs, first bring a large pan of water to the boil. Add all but two teaspoons of the vinegar and season with salt. Then reduce to a very gentle simmer. Break the eggs into the water and simmer for 3-4 minutes, until just cooked but still soft on the inside. Carefully remove with a slotted spoon and drain well on kitchen paper, trimming away any ragged edges.

Meanwhile, heat a frying pan and then add a tablespoon of the olive oil. Add the black pudding and cook for one minute on each side, until tender. Transfer to a plate lined with kitchen paper and keep warm. Snip the bacon into thin strips into the frying pan. Increase the heat a little and sauté for 3-4 minutes, until sizzling and lightly golden, tossing occasionally. Remove with a slotted spoon and drain on kitchen paper.

Pour the remaining two teaspoons of the vinegar into the pan, being careful of any spitting fat. Turn up the heat and scrape the sediment in the pan with a wooden spoon to deglaze for about 30 seconds, until almost all the vinegar has been boiled off. Stir the mustard into the reduced-down vinegar with the honey and then pour everything into a small bowl. Whisk in the rest of the olive oil, until you have achieved a nice thick dressing. Season to taste.

Meanwhile, place the salad leaves in a large bowl. Break the black pudding into pieces and scatter with the bacon over the salad. Drizzle over the dressing. Toss lightly to combine and arrange on plates. Top each one with a poached egg and a grinding of black pepper to serve. Hand around a basket of crusty bread separately.

Starters and Soups

Mixed bruschetta platter

Bruschetta makes delicious simple nibbles and can look very impressive laid out on platters. Alternatively use slices of French batons to make little bruschetta (crostini). Don't be tempted to make this too far in advance as the bread goes soggy.

INGREDIENTS
SERVES 4-6

12 thick slices country bread
1 garlic clove, halved
4 tbsp extra-virgin olive oil

Preheat the grill or a griddle pan and use to toast the bread on both sides. Remove from the heat and immediately rub one side with a piece of garlic. Drizzle over the olive oil and cut the slices of bread in half if they are very large.

Use immediately with a selection of the delicious toppings listed below. Arrange on large serving platters or trays to serve.

METHOD

GOAT'S CHEESE AND ONION MARMALADE

Heat two tablespoons of olive oil in a large pan and sauté three thinly sliced red onions until softened. Stir in 225g (8oz) of finely chopped ready-to-eat dried figs, two crushed garlic cloves, a glass of red wine and two tablespoons of balsamic vinegar. Simmer for about 10 minutes, until most of the liquid has evaporated, then stir in a teaspoon of caster sugar and a good pinch of chopped, fresh thyme. Season to taste and leave to cool completely, then spread onto the bruschetta and arrange thinly-sliced goat's cheese on top. Flash under the grill until the goat's cheese has melted.

ARTICHOKE & PARMESAN PURÉE

Place the contents of a 300g drained jar of artichoke hearts in a food processor with a handful of flat-leaf parsley leaves, 50g (2oz) of freshly grated Parmesan and a squeeze of lemon juice. Blitz to form a smooth paste and then, with the motor running, slowly add three tablespoons of extra-virgin olive oil, until well combined. Season to taste and spread thickly over the bruschetta.

PARMA HAM WRAPPED ASPARAGUS WITH TAPENADE

To make a rough textured tapenade, simply mix 250g (9oz) chopped pitted black olives in a bowl with the juice of a lemon, three tablespoons of chopped capers, six chopped anchovy fillets, one crushed garlic clove and two tablespoons of chopped fresh flat-leaf parsley. Season to taste and add enough extra-virgin olive oil to form a thickish paste. Spread 12 slices of Parma ham with some of the tapenade and then use to wrap 12 blanched asparagus spears. Spread the rest of the tapenade over the bruschetta and top with the Parma ham-wrapped asparagus rolls.

WILD MUSHROOM STRUDEL

This is a very impressive vegetarian starter that contains a wonderful combination of sautéed mushrooms and a crisp pastry crust. The filo pastry helps to keep the mushroom mixture really moist and full of flavour. The strudel can be prepared several hours in advance as long as it is tightly covered with clingfilm in the fridge and just popped in the oven once your guests arrive.

INGREDIENTS
SERVES 4-6

2 tbsp olive oil, plus extra for greasing
2 garlic cloves, crushed
1 small onion, finely chopped
225g (8oz) mixed wild mushrooms (eg: chanterelle, shiitake and oyster), roughly chopped
1 bunch spring onions, trimmed and chopped
2 tbsp chopped fresh mixed herbs (such as basil, parsley and chives)
4-5 sheets filo pastry, thawed if frozen (about 100g (4oz) in total)
1 egg, beaten
salt and freshly ground black pepper
lightly dressed mixed salad leaves and warm crusty bread, to serve

METHOD

Preheat the oven to 190°C (375°F), Gas mark 5. Heat the olive oil in a large frying pan. Add the garlic, onion and mushrooms and cook over a high heat for 2-3 minutes until almost tender. Add the spring onions, herbs and seasoning to taste. Sauté for another minute until the spring onions are just tender and the liquid has almost completely reduced. Leave to cool.

Unroll the sheets of filo pastry and place them one on top of the other on a work surface. Brush the surface of the top sheet of pastry with beaten egg and then spread over mushroom mixture to within 4cm (1½in) of the edges. Fold the short ends inwards and then starting with one long edge, roll up the pastry fairly tightly like you would a Swiss roll, keeping the mushrooms in place as you go.

Place the strudel seam-side down on a lightly greased baking sheet and brush once more with the rest of the beaten egg.

Bake for 20-25 minutes until crisp and golden brown.

Leave to cool for a few minutes before sliding off the baking sheet onto a chopping board. Cut the strudel across into 10-12 x 4cm (1 ½in) thick slices on the diagonal and arrange on warmed plates with some dressed mixed salad leaves and crusty bread, if liked.

GOAT'S CHEESE PUFF PIZZA WITH ROCKET

Instead of using the normal yeast dough in this pizza, I've made it with puff pastry. This is not as difficult as it sounds because, like a lot of people, I have discovered that you can buy this wonderful pastry ready-made in the frozen-food department of your supermarket.

INGREDIENTS
SERVES 4

500g packet frozen puff pastry, thawed
1 egg, beaten with a little milk
4 tbsp olive oil
1 small red and yellow pepper, cored, seeded and diced
1 small courgette, trimmed and diced
½ small aubergine, trimmed and diced
2 garlic cloves, crushed
2 plum tomatoes, peeled, seeded and diced
1 tsp tomato purée
1 tbsp chopped fresh basil
100g (4oz) hard goat's cheese
3 tbsp basil pesto (see recipie p.126)
handful wild rocket leaves
salt and freshly ground black pepper

METHOD

Roll out the pastry to a thickness of about 5mm (¼in) and cut out 4 x 15cm (6in) rounds. Arrange on two large baking sheets and put into the fridge for at least 30 minutes to rest.

Preheat the oven to 190°C (375°F), Gas mark 5. Prick the surface of each pastry base with a fork (this prevents the pastry from bubbling up or rising too much). Place in the oven to cook for 10-15 minutes until golden brown, swapping the baking sheets halfway through to ensure the pastry bases cook evenly. Remove from the oven and brush each pizza base with some eggwash to seal the pastry.

Meanwhile, heat the half the oil in a frying pan. Add the pepper, courgette and aubergine and sauté for about 5 minutes until almost tender. Season to taste and set aside.

Heat the rest of the olive oil in a separate frying pan, then sauté the garlic, tomatoes, tomato purée, basil until the tomatoes have softened. Season to taste. Spread some tomato sauce on each pizza base and then divide the vegetable mixture on top. Crumble over the goat's cheese and drizzle with half of the pesto. Return to the oven for 6-8 minutes or until the goat's cheese is bubbling and lightly golden.

Place each pizza on a plate and drizzle the rest of the pesto around the edge of each plate. Scatter around the rocket before serving.

Smoked salmon rolls with cream cheese and red onion

This is a great starter that is really easy to make and can be made ahead of time, which is always handy. They also make great canapés for a party. When buying smoked salmon, make sure you know what you're really getting. Irish smoked salmon may only be smoked in Ireland, but "smoked Irish salmon" is definitely Irish; and, in my opinion, it's the best.

Ingredients
Serves 4

1 red onion, finely diced
350g (12oz) pre-sliced Irish smoked salmon
75g (3oz) soft cream cheese
2 tbsp crème fraîche
1 tbsp snipped fresh chives
8 large slices wheaten bread
1 lemon (½ finely grated rind and ½ sliced for garnish)
25g (1oz) rocket leaves
salt and freshly ground black pepper

Method

Place the red onion in a small bowl and pour over enough boiling water to cover, then drain off immediately. This softens the raw flavour of the onion.

Return the red onion to the bowl and add the cream cheese, crème fraîche and chives. Season to taste and mix well to combine.

On a sheet of clingfilm, place three overlapping slices of smoked salmon. Spread the cream cheese mixture a few millimetres thick over the top of the salmon, right out to the edges. Roll up into a neat sausage shape. Repeat this process with the remaining slices and keep chilled in the fridge until ready to serve

Using a straight-sided scone cutter that is about 5cm (2in) in diameter, cut out two rounds from each slice of wheaten bread (use the leftovers in brown bread ice cream).

Slice each chilled smoked salmon roll into 4 small rounds. Place a wheaten bread round on a plate and arrange the smoked salmon slices on top. Garnish with some lemon rind and rocket leaves. Serve with the lemon slices.

Melon, orange and mint salad

This salad makes a refreshing starter at any time of the year but particularly at Christmas when pomegranates are in plentiful supply. Use the sweetest oranges you can find and make sure you take the time to remove all the bitter pith before cutting them into segments.

Ingredients
Serves 6

3-4 large oranges
1 honeydew melon
1 large pomegranate, seeds removed
2 tbsp extra-virgin olive oil
6 tbsp freshly squeezed orange juice
handful fresh mint leaves
salt and freshly ground black pepper

Method

To get lovely slices of orange without any bitter pith, take a slice off the bottom and top of the orange, then carefully cut away the skin and pith, following the curve of the orange. Continue along the orange, until you have removed all the peel and pith. Cut the orange into slices and repeat with the remaining oranges. Reserve any juice for the dressing.

Halve the melon and remove seeds. Using a melon baller, cut out balls. Alternatively, you may cut the melon into small cubes.

Arrange the orange slices in a martini or serving glass or on a plate. Add the melon balls and sprinkle with the pomegranate seeds. Whisk together the olive oil and orange juice, along with any pomegranate juice, then season to taste. Drizzle the dressing over the salad, then roughly tear the mint leaves and scatter on top to serve.

CHICKEN LIVER PÂTÉ WITH ONION JAM

I know how easy it is to buy pâté these days, but nothing tastes as good as homemade. This recipe can be prepared ahead and will keep for three to four days in the fridge.

INGREDIENTS
SERVES 6

400g (14oz) fresh chicken livers, trimmed
300ml (½ pint) milk
225g (8oz) unsalted butter
3 shallots, finely chopped
1 garlic clove, crushed
½ tsp chopped fresh thyme
1 tbsp port
4 eggs
1 tbsp cream

FOR THE ONION JAM:
25g (1oz) butter
2 red onions, thinly sliced
3 tbsp red wine vinegar
75ml (3fl oz) red wine
50g (2oz) soft brown sugar
salt and freshly ground black pepper
toast triangles and lightly dressed salad leaves, to serve

METHOD

To make the pâté, soak the chicken livers in a bowl of milk overnight in the fridge. The next day drain off the milk and rinse under cold running water, then dry thoroughly with kitchen paper.

Heat a frying pan and then add 25g (1oz) of the butter. Tip in the shallots garlic, thyme and cook for a couple of minutes until softened. Sprinkle over the port and cook for another minute to burn off the alcohol. Remove from the heat and leave to cool. Melt 75g (3oz) of the butter and set aside to cool a little.

Preheat the oven to 160°C (325°F), Gas mark 3. Purée the chicken livers in a food processor for about 3 minutes until well blended. Add the shallot mixture and blend again for 30 seconds. Through the feeder tube add the eggs, cream with the reserved melted butter. Blend again briefly and then season generously.

Pass the chicken liver mixture through a sieve and pour into a 450g (1lb) loaf tin that has been lined with clingfilm (or you could use a Pyrex dish). Cover tightly with tin foil and place in a roasting tin half filled with hot water (otherwise known as a bain marie). Place in the oven for about 1 hour or until set. Leave to cool and put in the fridge for 1-2 hours to chill down or overnight is best.

Melt the remaining 100g (4oz) of butter in a small pan and then pour into a jug. Leave to cool a little and settle. Pour a layer over the set chicken liver pate, leaving behind any milky white sediment. This will preserve the pate.

To make the onion jam, melt the butter in a heavy-based saucepan. Add the onions, vinegar, red wine and sugar. Sauté for 5 minutes, tossing occasionally. Sprinkle over a tablespoon of water, then reduce the temperature and cook gently for 25-30 minutes. The onions should make a soft, sticky sweet and sour jam. Season to taste and leave to cool.

To serve, carefully remove the layer of butter which has preserved the pate and then scoop out spoonfuls or cut into slices and arrange on plates with the onion jam, toast triangles and salad leaves.

ROASTED ROOT VEGETABLE SOUP

This recipe for roasted root vegetable soup, as we say in Cavan, has eating and drinking in it. It is good, wholesome food with great fresh vegetables. If you are keeping an eye on the fat content, you could leave out the cream. With some brown bread, this makes for a very nourishing snack in the middle of the day. You can substitute pumpkin, turnip or celeriac for the swede, or just use a mixture – this is a very flexible recipe. If you don't add the cream as you're watching the calories, you might need a little extra stock to thin down the soup a little.

INGREDIENTS
SERVES 4

1 small swede (turnip), cut into cubes
2 carrots, cut into cubes
1 parsnip, cut into cubes
3 tbsp olive oil
1 onion, finely chopped
2 celery sticks, finely chopped
1 garlic clove, crushed
1 tsp chopped fresh thyme
1.2 litres (2 pints) vegetable stock
150ml (¼ pint) cream
salt and freshly ground black pepper

METHOD

Preheat the oven to 200ºC/400ºF/Gas 6. Place the swede, carrots and parsnip into a roasting tin and drizzle over two tablespoons of the olive oil. Season generously and roast for 25-30 minutes until golden brown and tender, shaking the tin occasionally to ensure even cooking.

Meanwhile, heat the remaining tablespoon of olive oil in a large, heavy-based pan and add the onion, celery, garlic and thyme. Stir well to combine, then fry for 4-5 minutes, until softened but not browned, stirring occasionally.

Add the roasted root vegetables to the pan, and pour in the stock. Bring gently to the boil, then reduce the heat, cover and simmer for 25-30 minutes until completely tender, stirring occasionally. Purée with a hand blender until completely smooth, or use an electric blender if you want a more chunky soup. To serve, stir the cream into the soup. Gently heat through and season to taste, then ladle into warmed bowls.

SPRINGTIME MINESTRONE

Minestrone is a classic Italian dish. It is quick and healthy with lots of texture. You can add other things, like the leftovers from roast chicken, but do use some discretion. Minestrone is not a dumping ground for whatever is in the fridge.

INGREDIENTS
SERVES 4

200g (7oz) mixed green vegetables (such as asparagus, courgettes and spring onions)
700ml (1 ¼ pints) vegetable stock
150g (5oz) cooked pasta (spaghetti works well, chopped into small pieces)
400g can butter beans, rinsed and drained
3 tbsp basil pesto (see recipie p.126)
salt and freshly ground black pepper

METHOD

Place the green vegetables in a medium-size saucepan, then pour over the stock. Bring to the boil, then reduce the heat and simmer for 2-3 minutes until the vegetables are cooked through but still retain a little bite.

Stir in the cooked pasta, beans and one tablespoon of pesto. Warm through, then ladle into warmed bowls and top each with another drizzle of pesto to serve.

BEETROOT BORSCHT

Broscht or Borsht is very popular in most parts of Eastern European and it was a Polish chef who was working in my kitchen who first introduced me to it. When choosing beetroot look for plump roots that are smooth and firm and avoid any that are showing signs of decay. I always grate them in a food processor to stop my hands from staining but if you have do them by hand you could always try wearing rubber gloves...

INGREDIENTS
SERVES 6

1 tbsp olive oil
1 leek, finely chopped
1 celery stick, finely chopped
275g (10oz) raw beetroot, peeled and finely grated
100g (4oz) potato, diced
150g (5oz) carrot, finely grated
1.2 litres (2 pints) beef or vegetable stock
2 tsp red wine vinegar
1 tsp sugar
about 3 tbsp soured cream
salt and freshly ground black pepper
dill sprigs, to garnish

METHOD

Heat the oil in a large pan, then fry the leek and celery for about 2-3 minutes, until softened but not coloured, while stirring occasionally. Add the beetroot, potato and carrot, stirring to combine.

Pour the stock into the pan, season and bring to the boil, then reduce the heat and simmer for about 40 minutes, or until the vegetables are completely tender and the soup has thickened slightly, stirring occasionally.

Season the soup to taste, then stir in the vinegar and sugar. Heat gently until the sugar has dissolved. Ladle the soup into warmed serving bowls and add a small dollop of soured cream, then garnish with the dill sprigs and serve immediately.

Bacon and cabbage soup

This is an especially wonderful combination. Try to use the freshest of cabbage and nice floury potatoes for a real treat and all you'll need is a hunk of moist, crusty bread for a complete meal.

Ingredients
Serves 4 – 6

50g (2oz) pearl barley
50g (2oz) butter
100g (4oz) rindless smoked bacon rashers, trimmed of excess fat and diced
125g (4 ½oz) potatoes, diced (about 1 medium)
1 small onion, finely chopped
1 garlic clove, crushed
1 tbsp chopped fresh thyme
1.2 litres (2 pints) chicken stock
275g (10oz) cabbage, cored and finely shredded salt and freshly ground black pepper crusty white bread or wheaten bread, to serve

Method

Place the pearl barley in a saucepan and cover with plenty of water. Add a pinch of salt and bring to a simmer then simmer gently for 1 ½ hours or until the pearl barley is tender. Drain and set aside until needed.

Place a heavy-bottomed saucepan over a medium heat, add the butter to melt and stir in the smoked bacon, potatoes, onion, garlic and thyme. Cover with a lid and cook on a low heat for 10 minutes, stirring occasionally.

Add the stock to the bacon mixture with the cooked pearl barley and bring slowly to the boil. Tip in the cabbage, reduce the heat and simmer for about 5 minutes, until the cabbage is just tender. Season to taste with salt and pepper and serve with crusty white bread or wheaten bread.

LAMB, BEEF AND GAME

THYME-SPICED ROAST RIB EYE OF BEEF WITH HORSERADISH CREAM

Rib eye of beef is a very nice cut. The little bits of fat give it great flavour and it is very easy to carve and serve. The traditional accompaniment is horseradish, and I love the little kick it gives.

INGREDIENTS

SERVES 8-10

2.25kg (5lb) boned and rolled rib eye of beef
450ml (3/4 pint) red wine
150ml (¼ pint) red wine vinegar
1 tbsp sugar
1 tsp ground allspice
2 bay leaves
1 tbsp chopped fresh thyme
2 tbsp black peppercorns, crushed

FOR THE HORSERADISH CREAM:

200ml (7fl oz) carton crème fraîche
4 tbsp horseradish sauce
1 tbsp snipped fresh chives
salt and freshly ground black pepper
roasted root vegetables, to serve

METHOD

Place the rib eye of beef in a large non-metallic dish. Pour the wine into a jug and add the vinegar, sugar, allspice, bay leaf and half of the thyme. Mix well together and pour over the beef, turning to coat the joint evenly. Cover loosely with clingfilm and leave to marinate in the fridge for at least 4 hours or up to two days is perfect, turning occasionally.

When ready to cook, preheat oven to 190°C (375°F), Gas mark 5. Lift the beef from the marinade, allowing excess to drip off. Mix the crushed peppercorns with the remaining thyme and press all over the surface of the beef to coat the surface as evenly as possible. Place in a roasting tin and roast for 1 hour and 20 minutes for medium rare. Cook for an extra 30 minutes if you prefer your meat more well done.

Meanwhile, make the horseradish cream; mix the crème fraîche, horseradish and chives together in a bowl. Season to taste, spoon into a serving dish and chill until needed. When the beef is cooked, transfer to a warmed platter and cover with tin foil, then leave to rest in a warm place for about 30 minutes. Carve into slices and arrange on warmed plates with the roasted root vegetables and hand around the bowl of horseradish cream at the table.

LEG OF LAMB WITH SALSA VERDE STUFFING

Ask your local butcher to bone the leg of lamb for you, but to leave the shank end intact. This not only improves the flavour, but also makes carving much easier. For a more pronounced flavour, stud the lamb all over with slivers of garlic and tiny rosemary sprigs.

INGREDIENTS

SERVES 4-6

1 leg of lamb, 2.25-2.75 kg (5-6 lb), boned, but with shank end left intact
175g (6oz) fresh white breadcrumbs
50g (2oz) bunch fresh flat-leaf parsley, leaves stripped and finely chopped
1 tbsp rinsed capers
4 anchovy fillets, drained and finely chopped
50g (2oz) proscuitto, finely chopped
1 garlic clove, crushed
1 tsp Dijon mustard
1 tbsp fresh lemon juice
50ml (2fl oz) olive oil

FOR THE GRAVY:

1 tbsp plain flour
1 tsp tomato purée
100ml (3½floz) red wine
50ml (2fl oz) balsamic vinegar
200ml (7fl oz) beef or lamb stock
3 tbsp redcurrant jelly
salt and freshly ground pepper

METHOD

Preheat oven to 190°C (375°F), Gas mark 5. To make the stuffing, place the breadcrumbs in a bowl and add the parsley, capers, anchovies, proscuitto and garlic. In a separate bowl, whisk together the Dijon, lemon juice and olive oil. Fold into the breadcrumb mixture and season to taste.

Press the stuffing inside the boned-out leg of lamb, then tie up securely and neatly with string. Place in a roasting tin and season all over. Cover loosely with foil and roast for 1 ½ hours, then remove the foil and baste well. Roast for another 30 minutes, until just tender. If you like your lamb more well done, give it another 30 minutes. To check that it is cooked to your liking, insert a skewer into the thickest part of the meat, then watch the juice run out – the pinker the juice, the rarer the meat. When it is cooked to your liking, transfer to a carving platter and leave to rest on a warm plate for 30 minutes.

To make the gravy, place the roasting tin on the hob and stir in the flour, then cook for 1 minute, stirring. Gradually stir in the tomato purée, wine, vinegar and stock, whisking until smooth and scraping the bottom to remove any sediment. Transfer to a small saucepan and whisk in the redcurrant jelly and then simmer for another few minutes. When the lamb is rested, cut away the string, then carve into slices, holding the shank end of the bone. Arrange on warmed plates and spoon over a little of the gravy to serve.

BRAISED LAMB SHANKS WITH BARLEY AND ROSEMARY

This is wonderful for cold days and perfect for serving when you want to relax and enjoy the company with no last minute hurdles. When buying the lamb shanks, ask your butcher to trim off any excess fat and remove the knuckles – it will save what can be a difficult job. They extremely good value for money so it's well worth seeking them out.

INGREDIENTS
SERVES 6

1 tbsp sunflower oil
6 lamb shanks, well trimmed and knuckles removed
200g (7oz) carrots, cut into wedges
1 onion, roughly chopped
4 garlic cloves, peeled
1 fresh thyme sprig, plus extra to garnish
1 fresh rosemary sprig
50g (2oz) pearl barley, washed
2 litres (3 ½ pints) beef stock
600ml (1 pint) red wine
12 baby onions, peeled
1kg (2 ¼lb) potatoes, cut into chunks
75g (3oz) butter
1 bunch spring onions, trimmed and finely chopped (about 6 in total)
salt and freshly ground black pepper

METHOD

Preheat the oven to 160°C (325°F), Gas 3. Heat oil in a large casserole with a lid over a high heat. Add the lamb shanks and fry until lightly browned on all sides, turning regularly. Transfer to a plate. Add the carrots, onion and garlic to the pan and sauté for 5 minutes until lightly golden. Tip into a bowl.

Return the lamb shanks to the casserole with the herbs and barley. Pour over the stock and wine to cover. Season to taste and cover tightly with foil and then the lid. Bake for 1 ½ hours. Remove the casserole from the oven, add the reserved vegetables and pearl onions and cook for another hour until the lamb is very tender and almost falling off the bone. Strain the cooking liquid into a separate pan and then put the lid back on the casserole to keep the lamb shanks warm. Bring the cooking liquid back to a simmer, then cook until reduced to a sauce consistency. Season to taste.

Meanwhile, cook the potatoes in a pan of boiling salted water for 15-20 minutes or until completely tender. Drain and mash until smooth. Melt the butter in a sauté pan over a medium heat and sauté the spring onions for 2-3 minutes until tender. Beat in the mashed potatoes and season to taste.

To serve, spoon the mashed potatoes on to warmed plates and arrange a lamb shanks on top of each one. Spoon the vegetables to the side and drizzle around the reduced sauce. Garnish with thyme sprigs.

LAMB CUTLETS WITH GARLIC, LEMON AND PAPRIKA

Lamb cutlets are that bit more expensive, but they take no time to cook. Or you can put them on the barbecue, and they are great to eat with your fingers. This marinade is wonderful with lamb and would also work well with any type of lamb-leg steaks or sideloin chops, depending on what is available. The longer you can marinade this, the better the flavour, so it is well worth preparing in advance. It also goes well with pork and chicken or, indeed, with a nice striploin steak.

INGREDIENTS
SERVES 4

2 lamb cutlets, well trimmed
2 tbsp olive oil
2 garlic cloves, crushed
finely grated rind and juice of 1 lemon
1 tsp ground paprika
2 tsp chopped fresh oregano or thyme
1 tsp clear honey
sea salt and freshly ground black pepper
peach, feta cheese and rocket salad and
crusty bread, to serve

METHOD

Place the olive oil in a shallow, non-metallic dish and add the garlic, lemon rind and juice, paprika, herbs and honey. Season to taste and stir until well combined. Add the lamb, turning to coat, then set aside for at least 10 minutes, or up to 24 hours, covered with clingfilm in the fridge if time allows.

When you are ready to cook it, light the barbecue or preheat a griddle pan until it's smoking hot. Shake the excess marinade from the lamb. Put the lamb on the barbecue on medium-hot coals or on to the griddle pan. Cook for 6-8 minutes, until cooked through, turning once. Remove from the heat and leave to rest for a couple of minutes. Serve the lamb on warmed plates with the salad and crusty bread.

SLOW COOKED SHOULDER OF LAMB

This is a great way to cook a shoulder of lamb and ensures succulent meat packed full of flavour every time. Ask your craft butcher to prepare the joint for you.

INGREDIENTS
Serves 4

2 tbsp sunflower oil
1.75g (4lb) lamb shoulder, well trimmed, boned and tied with string
200g (7oz) carrots, cut into wedges
12 baby onions, peeled
4 garlic cloves, peeled
1 fresh thyme sprig
2 fresh rosemary sprigs, plus extra to garnish
50g (2oz) pearl barley, washed
2 litres (3 ½ pints) beef stock
600ml (1 pint) red wine
salt and freshly ground black pepper
champ, to serve
chopped fresh flat-leaf parsley, to garnish

METHOD

Preheat the oven to 160°C (325°F), Gas mark 3. Heat half the oil in a large casserole dish with a lid, over a high heat. Add the lamb shoulder and fry for 3-4 minutes, until lightly browned on all sides, turning regularly. Transfer to a plate and set aside. Add the carrots, baby onions and garlic to the pan and sauté for about 5 minutes, until lightly golden. Tip into a bowl and set aside.

Return the lamb shoulder to the casserole with the herbs and barley. Pour over the stock and wine to cover and return to the boil. Season to taste and cover tightly first with foil and then the lid. Bake for 1 ½ hours. Remove the casserole from the oven. Add the reserved vegetables and cook for another hour, until the lamb is very tender and almost falling apart.

Lift the lamb out of the casserole and leave to cool. Remove the string and wrap tightly in tin foil. Place in fridge for 3-4 hours, or overnight if possible, as this helps the lamb to keep its shape. Leave the cooking juices to cool, then cover with a lid and chill until needed. Once chilled,

you can skim off all the solidified fat and strain the vegetables through a colander over a pan, reserving the vegetables. Bring the liquid to the boil, then reduce to a simmer and cook for 40-45 minutes until reduced by half, skimming any impurities that rise to the surface. Return the vegetables to the sauce and simmer for about 5 minutes until warmed through. Season to taste.

Remove foil from the lamb shoulder and trim off the ends to neaten. Slice into eight pieces, each about 2.5cm (1in) thick. Heat the rest of the oil in a frying pan and very gently sear the lamb for 3-4 minutes on each side, until golden brown and warmed through. Drain on kitchen paper. Spoon the champ into warmed bowls and arrange two pieces of lamb on top of each one. Spoon over the vegetables and sauce, garnish with parsley to serve.

BUTTERFLIED LEG OF LAMB WITH SPICED MINT AND YOGHURT RUB

This butterfly leg of lamb is the perfect choice for the barbecue but also works wonderfully in the oven. Your butcher will bone and butterfly it for you so that there is no waste at all. This lamb would also be nice served with a pile of warmed pita breads or flour tortillas in the centre of the table, so everyone can help themselves.

INGREDIENTS
SERVES 4-6

3kg (7lb) leg of lamb, boned and well trimmed, roughly 5cm (2in) thick
25g (1oz) chopped fresh mint
juice of 2 lemons
4 garlic cloves, finely chopped
2 tbsp ground coriander
1 tbsp mild chilli powder
2 tsp ground cumin
2 tsp coarse ground black pepper
4 tbsp extra-virgin olive oil
6 tbsp Greek strained yoghurt
salt and freshly ground black pepper
lightly dressed green salad, to serve

METHOD

Place the lamb in a shallow non-metallic dish. Mix together the mint in a bowl with the lemon juice, garlic, ground coriander, chilli powder, ground cumin, olive oil, yoghurt and a teaspoon of freshly ground black pepper. Rub all over the meat, then cover with clingfilm and chill overnight or leave to stand at room temperature for 2-3 hours if time is short.

Preheat the oven to 230°C (475°F), Gas mark 9 or light a barbecue. If the lamb has been chilled overnight, bring it back to room temperature. If cooking in the oven, place the lamb, cut side up on a rack in a large roasting tin and season with salt. Roast in for 15 minutes, then turn over and roast for another 10 minutes for rare. Barbecue over medium-hot coals for about 50 minutes for medium rare lamb, turning occasionally.

Remove the lamb from the oven or barbecue and leave to rest in a warm place for 10 minutes. If you don't like your lamb too pink you can cover it with foil at this point and it will continue to cook. Carve into slices and arrange on plates with some salad.

STUFFED BEEF ROLLS WITH RED WINE SAUCE

This recipe uses a good value cut that isn't as popular as it should be. It is perfect comfort food for the family and ideal for a cold winters day. This casserole does take time, because it needs slow cooking to get as much flavour as possible and to become very tender so when these stuffed beef rolls are fully done you could eat them with a spoon!

INGREDIENTS
SERVES 4

4 x 100g (4oz) slices lean topside of beef
2 tbsp rapeseed or olive oil
2 carrots, finely diced
1 onion, finely diced
2 celery sticks, diced
1 tbsp tomato purée
250ml (9fl oz) red wine
600ml (1 pint) beef stock
1 bay leaf
2 fresh thyme sprigs, plus extra sprigs to garnish.

FOR THE STUFFING:

1 tbsp olive oil
1 onion, finely chopped
2 tsp fresh thyme leaves
2 parsnips, grated
pinch curry powder
1 slice white bread
Mashed potatoes, to serve (optional)

METHOD

Start with the stuffing. Heat the oil in a sauté pan, add the onion and thyme and cook until soft. Add the grated parsnips and cook for 2-3 minutes. Stir in curry powder and cook for 20 minutes. Make breadcrumbs from the slice of bread and stir into parsnip mixture. Spread the mixture over the beef slices and roll them up to enclose, securing them with a cocktail stick.

Preheat oven to 180°C (350°F), Gas mark 4. To prepare the casserole, heat the oil in a casserole dish over a high heat and sear the beef parcels until brown all over. Remove to a plate and set aside.

Next, sauté the carrots in the casserole dish with the onion and celery for a few minutes until just catching colour. Add the tomato purée, wine, beef stock, bay leaf and thyme and bring slowly to the boil. Return the beef to the casserole, cover and cook in oven for 1-1 ½ hours. Season to taste.

To serve, remove the cocktail stick from the beef parcels and slice them. Arrange on warmed plates and pour over the sauce. Garnish with the thyme. Add a dollop of mashed potatoes to each one to serve.

BEEF AND BUTTON MUSHROOM CASSEROLE

This is a good base casserole and you can add different flavours each time to keep it interesting. It is great with diced, smoked bacon and two cloves of crushed garlic added. Don't forget, you can have a glass of red while you are making this. Or if you do not drink, another good possibility is to add diced shoulder pork and replace the red wine with apple juice.

INGREDIENTS
SERVES 6-8

2 tbsp olive oil
25g (1oz) butter
900g (2lb) topside or stewing beef, trimmed and cut into 2.5cm (1in) cubes
600ml (1 pint) red wine
1 tbsp tomato purée
900ml (1 ½ pints) beef or chicken stock (from stock cubes is fine)
1 bay leaf
1 tsp chopped fresh thyme
1 tbsp Worcestershire sauce
450g (1lb) button mushrooms, halved
225g (8oz) shallots, trimmed and peeled (with root intact)
salt and freshly ground black pepper
boiled floury potatoes, to serve

METHOD

Pre-heat the oven to 200°C (400°F), Gas mark 6. Heat half of the oil and butter in a heavy-based casserole with a lid over a high heat. When the butter is foaming, tip in about a quarter of the beef and cook for 3-4 minutes, stirring regularly with a wooden spoon to seal in the flavour. Transfer to a bowl with a slotted spoon and set aside. Repeat in batches until all of the meat has been browned, adding extra olive oil and butter as necessary.

Pour a quarter of the wine into the casserole and de-glaze with a wooden spoon by scraping the caramelised meat residue from the base. Stir in the tomato purée and mix thoroughly to combine. Return the beef to the casserole with the rest of the wine, the stock, bay leaf, thyme, Worcestershire sauce and season to taste. Bring to the boil, then cover and place in the middle of the oven for 1 hour 45 minutes, stirring every half an hour or so.

Reduce the oven temperature to 180°C (350°F), Gas mark 4. Take the casserole out of the oven and stir in the mushrooms and shallots, then return to the oven without the lid for 45 minutes until the meat and vegetables are completely tender and the liquid has nicely reduced. To serve, ladle the stew into warmed wide-rimmed serving bowls with boiled floury potatoes on the side to soak up the rich juices.

CLASSIC ITALIAN LASAGNE

This dish needs no introduction as the Irish have taken to it as if it was their own. This recipe makes two dishes as I figure if you are going to go to the trouble of making it you might as well freeze one or use to feed a crowd!

INGREDIENTS
SERVES 12

2 tbsp olive oil
1 large onion, finely chopped
1 large carrot, finely diced
100g (4oz) button mushrooms
2 garlic cloves, finely chopped
1 tsp chopped fresh thyme
675g (1 ½lb) lean minced beef
2 tbsp tomato purée
2 x 400g cans chopped tomatoes
50g (2oz) butter
50g (2oz) plain flour
900ml (1 ½ pints) milk
100g (4oz) Cheddar cheese, grated
14-16 lasagne sheets
salt and freshly grated black pepper

METHOD

To make the bolognaise sauce, heat a large saucepan. Add the oil with the onion, carrot, mushrooms, garlic and thyme. Cook for 8-10 minutes until the vegetables have softened and taken on a little colour, stirring occasionally. Add the minced beef and mix until well combined, then sauté until well browned, breaking up any lumps with a wooden spoon. Stir in the tomato purée and continue to cook for another minute or two, stirring. Pour in the tomatoes and season to taste. Bring to the boil, then reduce the heat to the lowest setting and simmer for 2 hours until the beef is meltingly tender and the sauce has slightly reduced.

To make the cheese sauce, melt the butter in a saucepan. Stir in the flour and cook for 1 minute, stirring. Remove from the heat and gradually pour in the milk, whisking until smooth after each addition. Season to taste. Bring the sauce to the boil, whisking constantly, then reduce the heat and simmer gently for 5 minutes until smooth and thickened, stirring occasionally. Remove from the heat and stir in most of the Cheddar cheese until melted.

To cook the lasagne, preheat the oven to 180°C (350°F), Gas mark 4. Line 2 x 2.25 litre (4 pint) ovenproof dishes with a layer of lasagne sheets, breaking them to fit as necessary. Add half of the bolognese and spread it into an even layer. Spread over half of the cheese sauce. Cover with another layer of the remaining lasagne sheets. Use the rest of the bolognese to make another layer and then pour over the remaining cheese sauce. Scatter the rest of the Cheddar on top and bake for 1 hour or until the lasagnes are bubbling and lightly golden. Serve straight to the table.

BRAISED PHEASANT WITH APPLES AND BABY ONIONS

A marvellous dish for this time of year, when pheasants come into season. Surprisingly enough, you can buy them in the supermarkets as well as from more conventional game dealers these days, and many fishmongers also sell pheasants. A cock pheasant, though slightly tougher than a hen, will feed four people, the hen by and large only three. Simply serve this with celeriac and potato mash-you don't need any other vegetable, as there are plenty in the casserole itself.

INGREDIENTS
SERVES 3-4

1 pheasant, cleaned and prepared
25g (1oz) butter
1 tbsp sunflower oil
1 large onion, finely chopped
4 celery sticks, finely diced
225g (8oz) carrots, chopped
4 tbsp red wine vinegar
300ml/½ pint red wine
bouquet garni (2 celery sticks, 1 bay leaf, 1 fresh thyme sprig, 4 fresh parsley stalks all tied together with string)
2 eating apples, peeled, cores removed and sliced
10 pickling-sized baby onions
2 tsp arrowroot or potato flour
salt and freshly ground black pepper
chopped fresh parsley, to garnish
celeriac and potato mash, to serve

METHOD

Preheat the oven to 180°C (350°F), Gas mark 4. Joint the pheasant or get your game dealer or butcher to do it for you. Heat the butter in the oil in an ovenproof casserole and brown the pheasant pieces over a high heat. Add the onion, celery and carrots and turn to coat in the juices. Pour in the vinegar, bring to the boil and allow to almost boil away. Season generously and pour in the red wine and add the bouquet garni. Return to the boil, cover and simmer for 25 minutes. Add the apples and baby onions and place in the oven for 20 minutes.

To serve, mix the arrowroot or potato flour into a little water to make a smooth paste and stir it into the casserole. Place on the hob and heat through until at boiling point when the sauce will thicken and clear. Sprinkle over the parsley and serve with celeriac and potato mash, making sure each person gets a portion of baby onions, apples and carrots as well as pheasant.

VENISON CASSEROLE

Casseroles are simply the easiest meals to prepare. First you do all your peeling, slicing and sautéing, then you pop everything into a large pot with a lid and leave it in the oven for a couple of hours. In the meantime, you can go for a walk, watch a movie, mow the lawn and, later on, you can settle down to a hearty, warming feast.

INGREDIENTS
SERVES 6

100g (4oz) butter
900g (2lb) venison haunch, cut into 2.5cm (1in) cubes
1 large onion, chopped
2 tbsp paprika
50g (2oz) plain flour
1 tbsp tomato purée
about 1.75 litres (3 pints) beef stock
225g (8oz) carrots, cut into chunks
675g (1 ½lb) potatoes, cut into chunks
6 tbsp milk
salt and freshly ground black pepper
chopped fresh flat-leaf parsley, to garnish

METHOD

Preheat oven to 180°C (350°F), Gas mark 4. Heat half of the butter in a large, heavy-based casserole dish. Season the venison and add to the dish. Add the onions and cook for 2 minutes, stirring. Stir in the paprika and flour, stirring to combine. Mix well and place in the oven for 10 minutes.

Remove the casserole dish from the oven and mix in the tomato purée. Add enough stock to cover the meat. Bring to the boil on top of the stove and season. Cover with a lid and return to the oven for 1 ½ hours. Then remove from the oven, add the carrots and continue cooking in the oven for another 30 minutes or until the meat and vegetables are tender.

Meanwhile, boil the potatoes, then drain and mash until smooth. Heat the milk in a small separate saucepan. Add the rest of the butter and then beat in the warmed milk. Season to taste. Place the mashed potatoes in warmed bowls and spoon over the venison casserole. Garnish with parsley and serve at once.

Poultry And Pork

CHICKEN, ROCKET AND PINE NUT PASTA

This pasta sauce for this recipe literally takes the time the pasta needs to cook. There is now a wide range of good quality pasta available but without a doubt my favourite is De Cecco that comes in blue packets and is now available in most larger supermarkets and good delis.

INGREDIENTS
SERVES 4-6

450g (1lb) penne pasta
6 tbsp pine nuts
3 tbsp olive oil
1 large onion, thinly sliced
2 garlic cloves, crushed
1 tsp fresh thyme leaves
4 boneless skinless large chicken breasts,
 sliced lengthways into thin strips (about
450g (1lb) in total)
2 tbsp wholegrain mustard
300ml (½ pint) cream
100g (4oz) wild rocket or watercress, tough
stalks removed
about 4 tsp chilli oil (optional)
salt and freshly ground black pepper
Parmesan cheese shavings, to garnish

METHOD

Plunge the penne into a large pan of boiling salted water and cook for about 10 minutes until 'al dente' or according to packet instructions.

Heat a frying pan over a medium heat and add the pine nuts. Cook for a few minutes until lightly toasted, tossing occasionally to prevent them from burning. Tip into a bowl and set aside.

Add two tablespoons of the oil to the frying pan and sauté the onion, garlic and thyme for 2-3 minutes until softened and just beginning to colour. Tip into a bowl and set side.

Add the remaining tablespoon of oil to the frying pan and then add the chicken strips. Cook for 2-3 minutes and season lightly, then turn over and cook for another 2-3 until cooked through and lightly golden. Return the onion mixture to the frying pan, stirring until well combined. Stir in the mustard and cream and then bring to a gentle simmer. Cook for 1 minute to just heat through but do not allow the mixture to boil.

Drain the pasta and quickly refresh, then return to the pan. Pour in the creamy chicken mixture and add the rocket or watercress. Toss lightly together to combine and season to taste. Divide among warmed bowls and sprinkle over the pine nuts. Drizzle over the chilli oil, if using and garnish with the Parmesan shavings to serve.

HONEY ROAST DUCK WITH RED CABBAGE AND APPLE

This would make a fantastic Sunday lunch or even an alternative family Christmas. Whatever the occasion the combination is always a winner. If the honey glaze seems to be thin once the duck has roasted, simply reduce it in the tin directly on the hob to a thick coating consistency. Pour over the duck and leave to rest for 15 minutes.

INGREDIENTS
SERVES 6

1.5kg (3lb) oven-ready duck (preferably Silver hill)
1 tsp crushed peppercorns
1 tsp coarse sea salt
5 tbsp clear honey

FOR THE RED CABBAGE:

1 tbsp sunflower oil
1 head red cabbage, finely sliced
2 tbsp balsamic vinegar
4 tbsp light brown sugar
300ml (½ pint) red wine
300ml (½ pint) apple juice
2 cooking apples, peeled, cored and chopped
1 tsp ground cinnamon
1 tsp mixed spice
1 tsp ground cloves
salt and freshly ground black pepper

METHOD

Preheat the oven to 160°C (325°F), Gas mark 3. Score the duck breast slightly, just cutting into the skin. Place the duck in a small roasting tin, rubbing the salt and pepper into the skin. Spoon over the honey, making sure it's completely covered. Place in the oven and roast for 2 ½ hours, basting occasionally with the honey and duck residue in the roasting tin. The honey will reduce to a wonderful sticky glaze and the duck should be meltingly tender.

Meanwhile, make the red cabbage; heat the oil in a heavy-based pan over a high heat. Add the cabbage, stirring to combine. Reduce the heat and cook for 15 minutes until the cabbage is well cooked down, adding a tablespoon or two of water if the cabbage starts to catch on the bottom. Add the vinegar, sugar, wine and apple juice. Give a good stir, then cover with a lid and simmer for 1 hour over a low heat, stirring occasionally. Stir in the apples and spices and cook gently for another 30 minutes, again stirring occasionally. Season to taste and keep warm over a low heat.

Remove the duck from the oven and transfer to a warmed platter for 15 minutes to rest. Carve into slices and arrange on warmed plates, discarding any excess fat. Add some braised red cabbage and apple to serve.

CHUNKY CHICKEN AND POTATO PIE

This recipe would be perfect to use for leftover turkey at Christmas, just omit chicken and cook as described below, folding in the turkey pieces before leaving the sauce to cool down. If you like a bit of kick to your food, try adding one teaspoon of cayenne pepper to the flour.

INGREDIENTS
SERVES 4-6

1 tbsp olive oil
4 large skinless chicken thighs, boned and trimmed
2 potatoes, cut into cubes
2 red onions, cut into wedges
2 leeks, trimmed and thickly sliced
2 garlic cloves, halved
1 bay leaf
1 tsp chopped fresh thyme
1 tbsp plain flour
50g (2oz) frozen peas
75g (3oz) button mushrooms, cut in half
300ml (½ pint) crème fraîche
300ml (½ pint) chicken stock
2 tbsp chopped fresh flat-leaf parsley
375g packet ready-rolled puff pastry, thawed if frozen
1 egg beaten (to glaze)
salt and freshly ground black pepper
fresh green salad, to serve

METHOD

Preheat the oven to 190°C (375°F), Gas mark 5. Put the olive oil in a roasting tin or large pie dish. Add the chicken thighs, potatoes, onions, garlic, bay leaf, thyme and flour. Toss well together and season to taste. Roast for 25 minutes until tender, turning the chicken and vegetables occasionally to ensure they cook evenly.

Remove from the oven and fold in the frozen peas, mushrooms, then stir in the crème fraîche, chicken stock and parsley. Leave to cool slightly.

Lay the pastry over the pie dish, tucking in the edges down the sides. Brush the rim with water to help it stick and then brush the top of pie with beaten egg to glaze. Bake in oven for 25-30 minutes or until pastry has risen and is golden and the chicken and vegetables are tender. Reduce temperature of the oven if browning too quickly.

To serve, bring the pie directly to the table and serve on to warm plates, handing a bowl of the fresh green salad around so that everyone can help themselves.

CHICKEN, MUSHROOM AND SMOKED BACON CASSEROLE

This is a very economical dish as it just uses chicken legs. However you could also use a whole oven-ready chicken and chop it into portions.

INGREDIENTS
SERVES 6

6 chicken legs
1-2 tbsp sunflower oil
175g (6oz) piece smoked bacon, cut into strips
1 onion, sliced
2 carrots, sliced
2 celery sticks, sliced
2 garlic cloves, finely chopped
1 bottle red wine
2 tsp chopped fresh thyme
500ml (18fl oz) chicken stock
25g (1oz) butter
18 baby onions or small shallots
250g (9oz) button mushrooms, quartered
2 tsp cornflour
salt and freshly ground black pepper

METHOD

Season the chicken legs. Heat one tablespoon of the sunflower oil in a casserole dish with a lid. Add the bacon and sauté for 3-4 minutes until lightly browned. Place in a bowl and set aside. Add half of the chicken, presentation-side down and cook for 3-4 minutes until golden brown, turning occasionally. Transfer to a plate and repeat with the rest of the legs.

Add another tablespoon of oil if necessary. Add the onion to the casserole dish with the carrots, celery and garlic and sauté for about 5 minutes until golden brown. Pour in the wine, add the thyme and bring to a simmer, then cook for 5 minutes, scraping the bottom of the pan to remove any sediment. Pour in the stock and return the chicken legs to the pan. Bring to a simmer, then cover and cook for about 1 hour or until the chicken legs are tender.

Meanwhile, melt the butter in a frying pan. Add the baby onions or shallots and sauté for 5 minutes. Scoop out with a slotted spoon and add to the bowl with the reserved bacon. Tip the mushrooms and sauté for 5 minutes until tender. Add to the bacon and onion mixture and set aside.

When the chicken is cooked, transfer to a plate and strain the sauce into a large saucepan, discarding the vegetables. Mix the cornflour with a little water, then whisk into the sauce. Return to the boil and then reduce to a simmer and cook for a few minutes until thickened, whisking occasionally. Stir in the bacon and onion mixture and simmer for 6-8 minutes until the flavours have had a chance to combine. Return the chicken, nestling it into the sauce and cook for another 5 minutes until heated through. Season to taste. Transfer to a warmed dish and serve straight from the table.

POT ROASTED CHICKEN WITH HERBY GARLIC BUTTER

Pot-roasting is a great way to keep chicken succulent and the bed of vegetables impart loads of flavour. I like this with a dollop of creamy mash, but that of course is up to you. It is worth buying good-quality chicken for this dish but this recipe works just as well with a guinea fowl or pheasant. The herby garlic butter is very flexible and is great with pasta. You could use it on its own or add some roast vegetables. It is also terrific with grilled fish. It will keep for two weeks in the fridge and freezes well too.

INGREDIENTS
SERVES 4

75g (3oz) butter
2 garlic cloves, crushed
2 tbsp chopped fresh mixed herbs (such as flat-leaf parsley, tarragon and basil)
1 tbsp olive oil
4 chicken breast fillets (skin on)
1 large leek, finely chopped
2 carrots, diced
3 celery sticks, diced
1 tsp chopped fresh thyme
6 tbsp dry white wine
3 tbsp chicken stock
salt and freshly ground black pepper
mashed potatoes, to serve

METHOD

Preheat the oven 160C (325F), Gas mark 3. To make the green butter, place the butter in a mini blender with the garlic, herbs and seasoning. Blend briefly and transfer to a small bowl with a spatula. Chill until needed.

Heat a casserole dish with a lid. Add the oil and then add the chicken breasts, skin-side down. Cook for a few minutes on each side until golden brown. Transfer to a plate.

Add the leek, carrots, celery and thyme to the pan and sauté for about 5 minutes until just starting to soften but not colour. Pour in the wine and allow to bubble down a little, then arrange the sealed chicken breasts on top. Cover with a lid and bake for another 20 minutes or until the chicken is tender.

Transfer the chicken breasts to a warm plate. Whisk two-thirds of the herby garlic butter into the vegetable mixture and spoon on to warmed plates. Arrange the chicken breasts on top and top each one with a scoop of the remaining butter. Add the mashed potatoes and serve at once.

PESTO STUFFED CHICKEN BREASTS WITH ROAST VEGETABLES

I always make our own pesto but I am sure plenty of you know the drill: pesto, pine nuts, garlic, Parmesan and olive oil or buy a good quality one.

INGREDIENTS
SERVES 4

125g ball mozzarella, torn into small pieces
4 tbsp basil pesto (see recipie p.126)
4 skinless, boneless chicken breast fillets
8 smoked streaky bacon rashers, rinds removed
8 cherry tomatoes

FOR THE ROAST VEGETABLES:

3 courgettes, trimmed and thickly sliced
3 carrots, cut into thick fingers
1 aubergine, trimmed and cut into thick fingers
3 garlic cloves, finely chopped
2 red peppers, cored, seeded and cut into chunks
2 large baking potatoes, peeled and cut into bite-sized chunks
1 onion, chopped
4 tbsp olive oil
2 tbsp balsamic vinegar
1 mild red chilli, seeded and finely chopped
1 tsp sesame seeds
salt and freshly ground black pepper

METHOD

Preheat oven to 200°C (400°F), Gas mark 6. To prepare the roast vegetables, place all of the vegetables in a large roasting tin and drizzle over the olive oil and balsamic vinegar. Then sprinkle the chilli and sesame seeds on top and season to taste. Spread everything out to a single layer, then roast for about 45 minutes until the vegetables are tender and catching around the edges, tossing once or twice.

Meanwhile, mix the mozzarella and pesto together. Cut a slit into the side of each chicken breast, then stuff with the pesto mixture. Place two halved cherry tomatoes in each breast. Wrap each stuffed chicken breast with two bacon rashers – not too tightly, but enough to hold the chicken together. Season, place on a baking sheet and place in the oven about 10 minutes after the vegetables went in. Roast the stuffed chicken breasts for 20-25 minutes or until the chicken is cooked through and tender and the bacon is crispy. Remove from the oven and rest in a warm place for 10 minutes.

Arrange the roast vegetables on warmed plates with the pesto stuffed chicken breasts to serve.

CREAMY BACON AND LEEK TART

This tart is packed full of flavour and something that all of the family should enjoy. If you find it difficult to make pastry or just don't have the time, try making it in the food processor. It literally takes minutes.

INGREDIENTS
SERVES 4

1 tbsp olive oil
175g (6oz) piece streaky smoked bacon, rind removed and cut into lardons
2 small leeks, trimmed and thinly sliced
2 eggs, plus 2 egg yolks
250ml (9fl oz) cream

FOR THE PASTRY:

100g (4oz) plain flour, plus extra for dusting
pinch of salt
50g (2oz) unsalted butter, chilled and cut into cubes, plus extra for greasing
1-2 tbsp iced water
1 egg yolk plus a little beaten egg, for glazing
salt and freshly ground black pepper
lightly dressed fresh green salad, to serve

METHOD

To make the pastry, place the flour, salt and butter in a food processor and blend until the mixture resembles fine breadcrumbs, then tip it into a large bowl. Gently mix in the iced water and egg yolk using a round-bladed knife until the pastry just comes together, then knead lightly on a floured surface for a smooth dough. Wrap in clingfilm and chill for at least 1 hour.

Roll out the pastry on a lightly floured as thinly as possible and use it to line a greased loose-bottomed 20cm (8in) fluted flan tin that is about 4cm (1 ½in) deep. If time allows chill the pastry case for 30 minutes to allow the pastry to rest and reduce shrinkage during cooking.

Preheat the oven to 180°C (350°F), Gas mark. Prick the pastry base with a fork, then line with a large piece of greaseproof paper or foil that is first crumpled up to make it easier to handle. Fill with baking beans or dried pulses and bake for 15 minutes until the case looks 'set' but not coloured.

Carefully remove the paper or foil and the beans from the 'set' pastry case, then brush the inside with a little beaten egg mixture to form a seal and prevent any leaks. Place back in the oven for a further 5-10 minutes until the base is firm to the touch and the sides are lightly coloured.

Reduce the oven temperature to 160°C (325°F), Gas mark 3. Heat a frying pan with the oil and lightly fry the bacon and leeks until the bacon is crisp and the leeks have softened, then spread out over the cooked pastry base. Place the eggs, yolks and cream in a bowl and whisk together until combined. Pour into the pastry case and bake for 35-40 minutes until just set and lightly golden. Serve hot or cold, cut into slices with some fresh green salad.

PORK CHOPS WITH ROSEMARY AND MUSHROOMS BAKED IN FOIL

Individual parcels can be made and served unopened to your guests. However, I find that making just a family size one is the handiest and gives excellent results. Serve with some plain boiled rice for a healthier option than the mashed potatoes.

INGREDIENTS
SERVES 4-6

1 tbsp olive oil
4-6 lean pork chops, well trimmed of excess fat (preferably saddle back)
knob of butter
1 red onion, thinly sliced
275g (10oz) chestnut mushrooms, sliced
4 tbsp crème fraîche
1 garlic clove, crushed
1 tsp Dijon mustard
1 tbsp chopped fresh flat-leaf parsley
good pinch chopped fresh rosemary (optional)
salt and freshly ground black pepper
mashed potatoes and wilted spinach, to serve (optional)

METHOD

Preheat the oven to 180°C (350°F), Gas mark 4. Take a large piece of foil, fold in half and place on a baking sheet. Heat the olive oil in a pan, quickly sear the chops on both sides until golden brown. Place side by side on the folded foil.

Melt the butter in the pan, stir in the onion and mushrooms, then sauté for a few minutes until tender and season to taste. Scatter over the pork chops. Mix the crème fraîche in a small bowl with the garlic, Dijon mustard, parsley and rosemary, if using, then drizzle over the chops.

Seal the edges of the foil together with a double fold, making sure that there will be plenty of room for expansion. Bake for 30 minutes until the parcel has puffed up and the pork chops are completely tender inside.

To serve, open the parcel at the table for that special effect and serve the pork chops on warmed plates, spooning over all the lovely juices. Add some mashed potatoes and wilted spinach, if liked.

ROAST PORK LOIN WITH SAGE AND ONION STUFFING

For the best crackling it is important not to baste the rind during cooking. If the joint is cooked and the crackling still isn't crispy enough for you, snip into strips with a scissors and flash under the grill.

INGREDIENTS
SERVES 6-8

75g (3oz) butter
1 large red onion, finely chopped
1 garlic clove, crushed
25g (1oz) pine nuts
125g (4 ½oz) fresh white breadcrumbs (day-old)
2 tsp chopped fresh sage
2 tsp chopped fresh flat-leaf parsley
1.75kg (4lb) boneless pork loin, skin scored at 5mm (¼in) intervals
1 tbsp olive oil
coarse sea salt and freshly ground black pepper

METHOD

Preheat oven to 200°C (400°F), Gas mark 6. Melt the butter in a large pan and gently fry the onion and garlic for 3-4 minutes until softened but not coloured, stirring occasionally and then remove from the heat. Meanwhile, heat a separate small frying pan and toast the pine nuts, tossing occasionally to ensure they colour evenly. Stir the breadcrumbs into the onion mixture with the sage and parsley. Tip in the toasted pine nuts and season to taste, mixing to combine. Leave to cool completely.

Place the pork joint skin-side down, on a board and run a sharp knife between the loin and the streaky part to separate them. Continue to cut under the loin part for about an inch, releasing it a little from the fat on the bottom. Gather the cool stuffing up, press it into a large sausage shape and then insert it into the opened up area, pressing it in to fit snugly. Close the opening over and then roll up the joint and tie with string at 2.5cm (1in) intervals to secure.

Turn the joint skin side up and transfer to a rack set in a large roasting tin and pat the skin dry with kitchen paper and then rub the olive oil into the skin with one tablespoon of sea salt. Cover with foil and roast for 20 minutes. Reduce the heat to 180°C (350°F), Gas mark 4 and roast for another 15 minutes and then remove the foil and cook for another 1 ¼ hours or until the pork is tender and the crackling is crisp and golden.

When the pork is cooked, transfer to a warmed serving plate, removing the rack from the roasting tin and leave the joint to rest, uncovered for about 20 minutes. Cut the string from the rested pork joint and cut through the fat just underneath the crackling. Remove and cut into pieces and then carve the pork into thick slices. Arrange on plates to serve.

PORK SAUSAGES WITH LEEK AND PARSNIP MASH

We all adore sausage and mash – it has to be one of my favourite comfort foods. Experiment with the type of pork sausage you use – most butchers and supermarkets now have a wide range of premium lines available.

INGREDIENTS
SERVES 6)

12 large pork sausages (good quality)
2 tbsp redcurrant jelly
1 tsp fresh lemon juice
2 tbsp olive oil
400g (14oz) onions, chopped
2 tbsp red wine vinegar
2 tbsp soft brown sugar
1 tbsp dark soy sauce

FOR THE LEEK AND PARSNIP MASH:

675g (1 ½lb) leeks, sliced
675g (1 ½lb) parsnips, quartered
1 garlic clove, peeled
100ml (3 ½fl oz) milk
1 tbsp chopped fresh parsley
1 tbsp freshly grated Parmesan cheese
salt and freshly ground black pepper

METHOD

Preheat the oven to 200°C (400°F), Gas mark 6. Place the sausages in a small roasting tin. Mix together the redcurrant jelly and lemon juice in a small bowl and spoon it over the sausages, then roast for 35 minutes until tender and cooked through, turning them once halfway through the cooking time.

Meanwhile, place the leeks, parsnips and garlic in a pan of salted water. Bring to the boil, then reduce the heat and simmer for 15-20 minutes or until the parsnips are completely tender. Drain and return to the pan to allow them to dry them out for 5 minutes over a low heat.

Heat the olive oil in a frying pan and gently fry the red onions for 15 minutes, turning regularly until softened but not coloured.

Add the vinegar, sugar and soy sauce and cook for another 5 minutes until the onions are really tender. Season to taste.

To finish the mash, heat the milk in a pan until it is warm, then pour into a food processor or liquidiser. Add the leeks, parsnips and garlic mixture with the parsley and Parmesan. Blend until smooth, then return the purée to the pan and reheat over a low heat until completely warmed through.

Arrange the leek and parsnip mash on warmed plates and place the sausages to the side. Add a dollop of the onion marmalade to serve.

VEGETARIAN

Butternut squash and pasta bake	79
Cheese, tomato and basil macaroni	80
Field mushrooms with spinach, blue cheese and caramelised red onion	81
Oriental vegetable and basil curry	83
Courgette and parmesan röstis with tomato dressing	85
Roasted peppers with Boilie cheese	87
Aubergine and mozzarella parcels with pesto	89
Salad selection plate	90

*(chunky potato salad, Puy lentil, red onion and sun-dried
tomato salad and Three-tomato salad with basil)*

BUTTERNUT SQUASH AND PASTA BAKE

The roasted butternut squash adds a wonderful zap to this pasta gratin, while the mascarpone cheese helps to keep everything really moist. This dish can be prepared several hours in advance and just popped into a preheated oven 180C (350F), Gas mark 4 from cold for 25-30 minutes or until heated through, then flash under the grill until bubbling.

INGREDIENTS
SERVES 6

1 tbsp olive oil
25g (1oz) butter, plus extra for greasing
1 butternut squash (about 675g
(1 ½lb) in total)
4 fresh rosemary sprigs
1 red onion, sliced
175g (6oz) chestnut mushrooms, sliced
275g (10oz) penne pasta
250g tub mascarpone cheese
50g (2oz) freshly grated parmesan cheese
salt and freshly ground black pepper
lightly dressed fresh green salad,
to serve

METHOD

Preheat the oven to 200°C (400°F), Gas mark 6. Place the oil and butter in a large roasting tin and heat for 3-4 minutes in the oven until the butter has melted. Peel the butternut squash and then cut in half and remove seeds; discard. Cut flesh into bite- sized chunks and then tip them into the heated butter and oil, tossing to coat. Season to taste and roast for 10 minutes. Stir in the rosemary, onion and mushrooms until well combined and roast for another 10 minutes or until all the vegetables are tender and just beginning to char.

Cook the pasta in a large pan of boiling salted water for about 10 minutes or according to packet instructions until 'al dente'.

Remove the roasting tin from the oven and stir in two tablespoons of water, then stir in the mascarpone cheese. Drain the pasta and tip into the roasting tin, stirring

to combine. Season to taste. Transfer to a buttered ovenproof dish and sprinkle over the Parmesan. Bake for another 10 minutes until bubbling and lightly golden.

Sprinkle the butternut squash pasta bake and place directly on the table, allowing people to help themselves on to warmed plates. Put the salad in a separate bowl on the table.

CHEESE, TOMATO AND BASIL MACARONI

This is the kind of pasta dish I tend to make when there's nothing much left in the fridge. It really takes no time to prepare and is great served with a light rocket salad and a decent glass of wine.

INGREDIENTS
(SERVES 4)

300g (11oz) cherry tomatoes on the vine
1 garlic clove, finely chopped
1 tbsp olive oil
350g (12oz) macaroni pasta
250g tub mascarpone cheese
2 tsp Dijon mustard
2 tbsp shredded fresh basil
200g freshly grated Parmesan cheese
salt and freshly ground black pepper

METHOD

Preheat oven 220°C (425°F), Gas mark 7. Carefully remove the cherry tomatoes from the vine and place in an ovenproof dish. Sprinkle with half the garlic and drizzle over the olive oil. Season to taste. Roast for 15 minutes until the tomatoes have softened slightly and skins have started to split, tossing once or twice to ensure even cooking.

Meanwhile, cook the macaroni in a large pan of boiling salted water and cook for 8-10 minutes or according to packet instructions until 'al dente' (tender but firm to the bite).

Place the mascarpone in a bowl and beat in the mustard, basil, Parmesan and the remaining garlic.

Drain the pasta and return to the pan. Stir in the mascarpone cheese mixture, then carefully fold in the roasted cherry tomatoes. Season to taste. Tip into the ovenproof dish that you used for the tomatoes. Bake for 20 minutes until bubbling and golden brown.

To serve, leave the cheese, tomato and basil macaroni to stand for a few minutes, then serve straight from dish on to warmed plates.

FIELD MUSHROOMS WITH SPINACH, BLUE CHEESE AND CARAMELISED RED ONION

Obviously these are fantastic served with some crusty bread to pop up all of the delicious juices but you could also serve it on a bed of roasted garlic mash for a more substantial vegetarian main course.

INGREDIENTS
SERVES 4-6

3 tbsp olive oil
450g (1lb) spinach, washed and stalks removed
2 garlic cloves, crushed
1 red onion, finely diced
6 baby vine ripened tomatoes, cut in half
25g (1oz) toasted pine nuts or walnuts
8 large field mushrooms, wiped clean (evenly-sized)
100g (4oz) mild blue cheese, diced (such as Cashel blue)
salt and freshly ground black pepper

METHOD

Preheat oven to 230°C (450°F), Gas mark 8. Heat one tablespoon of the olive oil in a large pan, add the spinach and stir fry over a high heat until just wilted. Tip out on to a layer of kitchen paper to absorb excess liquid. Place spinach on a chopping board and chop roughly. Place in a large bowl and set aside.

Add another tablespoon of olive oil to the pan and then add garlic and red onion. Cook for 5 minutes, until soft, stirring occasionally. Stir in the tomatoes and allow to just warm through. Gently fold into the spinach with the toasted pine nuts or walnuts and season to taste.

Remove stalks from mushrooms and keep for soup or discard. Brush with the remaining olive oil and place in a baking tin, gill side up. Season generously and bake for 5 minutes, then remove and spoon the spinach mixture on top. Scatter over the blue cheese and place back in oven for another 8-10 minutes until mushrooms are completely tender and cheese has melted and is bubbling. To serve, arrange on a warmed plates, spooning around any juices that are left in the pan.

ORIENTAL VEGETABLE AND BASIL CURRY

Some people love curry, and some are nervous about it. But this one is not too spicy, and if you make it a day before it tastes even better. It is a very versatile dish that also works well with beef or lamb. This curry is very quick and easy to prepare, especially now that most supermarkets sell authentic ready-made Thai curry pastes. Thai Gold is an Irish company and, for me, their paste is the best on the market.

INGREDIENTS
SERVES 4

2 tbsp sunflower oil
5cm (2in) piece fresh root ginger, peeled and into thin matchsticks
2 large garlic cloves, thinly sliced
2 heaped tbsp Thai red curry paste (look out for Thai Gold organic range)
400g can coconut milk
2 tsp soft brown sugar
juice of 1 lime
2 tbsp light soy sauce
300ml (½ pint) vegetable stock
1 small butternut squash, peeled, seeded and cut into cubes (about 350g (12oz) in total)
100g (4oz) fine green beans, trimmed and halved
100g (4oz) baby sweetcorn, halved lengthways
1 small red pepper, stalk and seeds removed, then cut into strips
15g (½oz) bunch fresh basil, leaves striped and chopped
steamed Thai fragrant rice, to serve

METHOD

Heat the oil in a large pan or wok. Add the ginger and garlic and cook gently for about 1 minute without browning, stirring. Add the curry paste and cook, stirring, for 2 minutes. Add the coconut milk, sugar, lime juice, soy sauce and stock and bring to the boil. Reduce to a simmer for 2 minutes until well combined, stirring occasionally.

Stir the butternut squash into the pan and simmer for 6 minutes. Add the green beans, sweetcorn and red pepper and simmer for another 5-6 minutes until all the vegetables are tender. Stir in the basil leaves and remove from the heat. Ladle into warmed deep bowls on top of some Thai fragrant rice to serve.

COURGETTE AND PARMESAN RÖSTIS WITH TOMATO DRESSING

As courgettes have a naturally high in water content it is very important that they get squeezed dry before using them in this recipe. This will ensure that the fritters are lovely and crisp, just as they should be.

INGREDIENTS
SERVES 4

550g (1 ¼lb) courgettes, coarsely grated
100g (4oz) ground rice
3 tbsp shredded fresh basil leaves, plus extra sprigs to serve
75g (3oz) freshly grated Parmesan cheese
1 egg, lightly beaten
50g (2oz) lightly toasted pine nuts
120ml (4fl oz) olive oil
1 ripe plum tomato, seeded and finely diced
4 sun-dried tomatoes, drained and finely chopped (preserved in oil)
1 small shallot, finely chopped
100g (4oz) wild rocket
salt and freshly ground black pepper

METHOD

Squeeze the courgette as dry as possible in a clean tea towel and tip into a large bowl. Mix in the ground rice, basil, Parmesan, egg and pine nuts. Season to taste and divide into 20 even-sized balls, then flatten slightly into patties

Heat one tablespoon of the olive oil in a large non-stick frying pan on a medium heat and carefully add half of the patties. Cook for 2-3 minutes on each side or until cooked through, crisp and golden. Drain on kitchen paper and keep warm. Repeat with another tablespoon of oil and the remaining patties.

To make the dressing; place the remaining oil in a bowl and add the plum tomato, sun-dried tomatoes and shallot and then season to taste. Stir until well combined. Divide the rocket among serving plates and drizzle over enough of the dressing to coat. Add the röstis, then drizzle around a little more dressing and garnish with the basil sprigs to serve.

ROASTED PEPPERS WITH BOILIE CHEESE

The Boilie cheese I use is produced at a local creamery Fivemiletown that is based in Fermanagh. Boilie are fresh cheese curds that have been rolled by hand into balls. They are readily available in jars and have been marinated in oil and herbs. There are two varieties, one coming from cow's milk and the other from goat's milk. Both have a wonderfully delicate flavour and are soft enough to spread. I just love them and like to use them here to fill red peppers, although the stalks of the peppers are not edible, they do look attractive and help the peppers keep their shape.

INGREDIENTS
SERVES 4

4 large red peppers
6 tbsp extra-virgin olive oil
4 ripe tomatoes
200g jar Boilie cheese, drained
Maldon sea salt and freshly ground black pepper
fresh basil leaves, to garnish
lighty dressed salad leaves, to serve

METHOD

Preheat your oven to 180°C (350°F), Gas mark 4. Cut the peppers in half and remove the seeds, but leave the stalks intact. Arrange the pepper halves in a lightly oiled baking tin.

Place the tomatoes in a bowl and pour boiling water over them. Leave them for one minute, then drain and peel the skins off. Cut into quarters and place two quarters into each pepper half.

Season the filled pepper halves and divide the remaining olive oil on top. Roast for 30-40 minutes, until the peppers are completely tender and lightly charred around the edges.

Preheat the grill. Place equal amounts of the Boilie cheese on top of the peppers.

Grill for 2-3 minutes or until cheese is lightly golden. Transfer the peppers to plates and spoon over all of the cooking juices. Garnish with fresh basil and serve with the salad leaves.

AUBERGINE AND MOZZARELLA PARCELS WITH PESTO

It's not without reason that aubergines are still regarded as the poor man's meat in the Middle East. They make an excellent vegetarian main course or light lunch, as they are so rich in nutrients. Prepare this in advance and simply pop in the oven just before you are ready to serve.

INGREDIENTS
SERVES 4

1 large aubergine
120ml (4fl oz) extra-virgin olive oil
2 garlic cloves, crushed
finely grated rind of 1 lemon
1 vine ripened beef tomato
2 x 125g balls mozzarella cheese
about 2 tbsp basil pesto (see recipie p.126)
8 semi sun-dried tomatoes, drained and
finely chopped (preserved in oil)
salt and freshly ground black pepper
lightly dressed rocket salad, to serve

METHOD

Trim off the stalk end of the aubergine and then cut lengthways into eight 5mm (¼in) thick slices, discarding the ends. Arrange the slices in a single layer on a large baking sheet, sprinkle lightly with salt and set aside for 30 minutes to one hour. This will make them easier to roll later on, as well as draw out some of the water.

Preheat a griddle pan until very hot, or light a barbecue. Rinse the aubergine pieces in cold water, then pat them really dry with kitchen paper. Mix together the olive oil, garlic, lemon rind and seasoning in a small bowl, then use some to brush all over the aubergine slices. Place on the heated griddle pan or a barbecue with medium-hot coals and cook for 2-3 minutes on each side, until charred. Set aside and leave to cool a little.

Cut the tomato into four thick slices, discarding the ends, then cut each slice in half again to make eight slices in total. Cut each mozzarella ball into four slices. Place the aubergine slices on a clean work surface and lay a piece of tomato in the middle of each slice. Arrange a slice of mozzarella on top, and then add a small dollop of the basil pesto. Sprinkle sun-dried tomatoes over the top and season with pepper.

Flip over both ends of each parcel to enclose the filling and secure each parcel with a cocktail stick. Brush the outside of each parcel with the rest of the garlic and lemon oil and return to the griddle pan or barbecue for one to two minutes on each side, or until they are heated through and lightly golden. Arrange on warmed plates with the rocket salad to serve.

SALAD SELECTION PLATE

In recent years, I have seen remarkable growth in the number of my customers choosing vegetarian meals. The days are gone when there was just one vegetarian option on the menu. Most restaurants now offer a good choice, and the range of vegetarian meals available has improved enormously. There is also a big increase in the number of people who are not fully vegetarian but sometimes like to cut down on their meat or fish. The vegetarian option is thought of as a healthy, low-calorie meal that is tasty and full of vitamins. These days, the farmers' markets have a large array of vegetables through the seasons. For the non-vegetarians among you, feel free to add some chicken, smoked salmon or ham to this selection of salads. The choice is yours.

THREE TOMATO SALAD

This tomato salad is very visual and the different varieties of tomatoes each have their own individual textures and flavours. Choose from the wide selection now available and tailor this salad to make it your own.

INGREDIENTS
SERVES 4

2 beef tomatoes, thinly sliced
4 ripe tomatoes, cut into wedges
100g (4oz) sunagold or baby plum cherry tomatoes, halved
1 shallot, thinly sliced
handful fresh basil leaves, shredded
6 tbsp French vinaigrette
freshly ground black pepper

METHOD

Arrange the beef tomatoes in a single layer on the base of a large serving plate, then scatter over the tomato wedges and finish with a pile of the cherry tomatoes. Sprinkle over the shallots and basil and then drizzle the vinaigrette on top. Add a good grinding of pepper and serve at once.

CHUNKY POTATO SALAD

This is also really good if you also stir in one finely chopped dill pickled cucumber and three finely diced hard-boiled eggs.

INGREDIENTS
SERVES 4

900g (2lb) small new potatoes, scraped or scrubbed
2 tsp white wine vinegar
2 tbsp olive oil
4 tbsp mayonnaise
2 tbsp crème fraîche or natural yoghurt
1 bunch spring onions, trimmed and thinly sliced
2 tbsp chopped fresh dill
2 tbsp chopped fresh flat-leaf parsley
salt and freshly ground black pepper

METHOD

If necessary, cut the potatoes into 2.5cm (1in) chunks. Place in a pan of salted water, bring to the boil and cook for 12-15 minutes or until tender. This will depend on your potatoes, so keep an eye on them.

Meanwhile, whisk together the white wine vinegar in a small bowl with the olive oil and season to taste. Drain the potatoes well, transfer to a serving bowl and gently stir in the dressing. Leave to cool completely.

Stir the mayonnaise and crème fraîche or yoghurt together in a small bowl and stir into the potatoes with the spring onions, dill, parsley and season to serve.

PUY LENTIL AND SUN-DRIED TOMATO SALAD WITH GOAT'S CHEESE

This has to be one of my favourite salads! It is as great to eat in the winter as it is in the summer. If you cover it with clingfilm it sits very well in the fridge so can be made well in advance and just brought back up to room temperature before eating.

INGREDIENTS
SERVES 4

225g (8oz) Puy lentils
4 tbsp extra-virgin olive oil
2 shallots, finely chopped
50g (2oz) sun-dried tomatoes, drained and finely chopped (preserved in oil)
175g (6oz) goat's cheese log, cut into small cubes
20g (1oz) fresh flat-leaf parsley leaves, roughly chopped
Maldon sea salt and freshly ground black pepper

METHOD

Rinse the lentils in sieve under cold running water, then place in a pan with 600ml (1 pint) of water. Add a pinch of salt and bring to the boil, then reduce the heat and simmer for 15-20 minutes or until 'al dente'- just tender but still with a little bite. Drain well.

Meanwhile, heat one tablespoon of the olive oil in a pan and sauté the shallots for 4-5 minutes until softened but not coloured. Tip into a salad bowl and stir in the cooked lentils with the rest of the olive oil and the sun-dried tomatoes.

When the lentils have cooled to room temperature, gently fold in the goat's cheese and parsley, then season to taste. Divide among plates to serve.

Family Favourites

ROCKET, MOZZARELLA AND PINE NUT PIZZA

Basic pizza dough is always nicer if you make it yourself. But there are lots of good pre-made pizza bases available to buy. The beauty of pizza is that the topping is not set in stone. You can mix and match as you like. Everyone has their own favourites. This basic tomato sauce is very versatile, and you can use it with pastas too. This sauce will keep for a week in the fridge or you can freeze it.

INGREDIENTS

MAKES ENOUGH FOR 16 SMALL OR
4 LARGE PIZZAS

4 x 125g balls mozzarella, roughly torn
4 tbsp toasted pine nuts
25g (1oz) wild rocket

FOR THE PIZZA DOUGH:

750g (1 3/4lb) strong bread flour, plus
extra for dusting
2 tsp salt
25g (1oz) butter, cubed
7g sachet dried yeast
350ml (12fl oz) lukewarm water

FOR THE TOMATO SAUCE:

1 tbsp olive oil
3 fresh tomatoes, roughly chopped
1 garlic clove, crushed
2 tbsp tomato purée
400g can chopped tomatoes
1 tbsp chopped fresh basil
salt and freshly ground black pepper

METHOD

First make the pizza dough. Mix the flour, salt, butter and yeast together in a large bowl or mixer. Carefully add the water bit by bit, until combined, to give a smooth, soft dough. Knead by hand for 10 minutes or in the mixer for 5 minutes. Leave to double in size in a warm place for about an hour. Knock back the risen dough by kneading again for a minute. Divide the dough into 16 equal sized pieces, and roll each one out on a floured surface with a rolling pin to give small individual pizza bases.

Preheat the oven to 220°C (450°F), Gas mark 7. To make the tomato sauce, heat the oil in a saucepan. Cook the fresh tomatoes, tomato purée and garlic for 4-5 minutes, stirring occasionally, until softened. Add the canned tomatoes and fresh basil. Simmer for 10 minutes, until the sauce has reduced slightly. Remove from the heat. Season to taste.

Arrange the pizza bases on baking sheets and spread over the tomato sauce, then scatter the mozzarella on top with the pine nuts. Bake for 8-10 minutes until the pizza bases are cooked through and the toppings are bubbling. Serve warm cut into wedges.

VARIATIONS

American Hot: prepare the bases with the tomato sauce and then scatter over 50g (2oz) of thinly sliced pepperoni and 50g (2oz) drained sliced jalapeños chillies (from a jar or can). Finish and serve as described above.

Garlic Mushroom and Parma Ham: sauté 50g (2oz) of sliced chestnut mushrooms with a crushed garlic clove in a little olive oil for a minute or two. Prepare the bases with the tomato sauce and then scatter over the mushrooms. Tear two to three slices of Parma ham or prosciutto on top. Finish and bake as described above, then remove from the oven and finish with a drizzle of olive oil and some Parmesan shavings before cutting into wedges to serve.

BEEF AND NOODLE STIR FRY

This stir fry has a lovely balance of flavours and textures for a quick no-nonsense yet healthy, tasty supper that all the family are sure to enjoy. Feel free to experiment with different kinds of noodles such as udon or rice noodles.

INGREDIENTS
SERVES 4

2 tsp sesame oil
2 garlic clove, peeled and sliced
4 x 100g (4oz) thin-cut sirloin steaks, trimmed and sliced into thin strips
75g (3oz) chestnut mushrooms, trimmed and sliced
2 carrots, thinly sliced
400g (14oz) medium egg noodles
150ml (¼ pint) chicken stock
2 tbsp light soy sauce
2 tbsp oyster sauce
2 tbsp sweet chilli sauce
2 tsp toasted sesame seeds

METHOD

Heat the sesame oil in a wok or large frying pan. Add the garlic and steak, then stir fry for 3 minutes until the meat is sealed. Add mushrooms and carrots, then cook for a further 5 minutes.

Meanwhile, bring a large saucepan of salted water to the boil. Add the noodles. Cook for 1 minute, or according to packet instructions, then drain and add to the beef and vegetable mixture in the wok, tossing to combine.

Add the chicken stock to the beef and noodle mixture with the soy sauce, oyster and sweet chilli and allow to heat through. Divide among warmed bowls and sprinkle with the sesame seeds to serve.

BAKED POTATOES WITH MINCE

The baked potato is undoubtedly the greatest standby meal. Choose a floury variety, such as Rooster or Maris Piper. You can give them a head start in the microwave on high for 5 minutes if your short of time, which halves the cooking time.

INGREDIENTS
SERVES 4

4 baking potatoes, each about 200g (7oz)
2 tbsp olive oil
1 onion, finely chopped
450g (1lb) button mushrooms, sliced
2 carrots, diced
1 garlic clove, crushed
450g (1lb) lean minced beef
2 tbsp Worcestershire sauce
300ml (½ pint) beef stock
1 tbsp tomato puré
1 tbsp milk
50g (2oz) butter
50g (2oz) mature Cheddar, grated
steamed green vegetables, to serve

METHOD

Preheat the oven to 180°C (350°F), Gas mark 4. Scrub the potatoes and pick with a fork then bake for about 1 hour until tender and cooked through.

Meanwhile, heat the oil in a frying pan. Add the onion and sauté for 2-3 minutes until softened. Add the mushrooms and carrots and sauté for another 2-3 minutes until the mushrooms are tender. Stir in the garlic and the mince, then cook for another 5 minutes or so until the mince has lost its pink colour, breaking up any lumps with a wooden spoon.

Stir the Worcestershire sauce into the mince mixture and cook for 2 minutes. Add stock and tomato purée, then cover and simmer for 20 minutes, until the mince is cooked through, and season to taste.

When the potatoes are cooked, cut them in half and scoop the flesh out into a bowl, leaving a thin layer in the shells. Add some seasoning to the cooked potato and then beat in the milk and butter until you have achieved a smooth mash.

Preheat the grill. Place the potato skins in a shallow roasting tin and spoon in the cooked mince mixture. Pipe or spoon the mashed potato on top. Sprinkle with the Cheddar cheese, then grill until cheese has melted and the filling is piping hot. Serve on warmed plates with some steamed green vegetables.

SAUSAGE CASSOULET

This dish originates from France and is simply delicious when made with good quality sausages. There is now a fantastic selection available and you can choose from fresh chorizo, venison or a more traditional pork and leek. Butter or borlotti beans would also work well for this recipe.

INGREDIENTS
SERVES 4

4 tbsp olive oil
8 pork and leek sausages
1 large onion, finely chopped
2 celery sticks, finely chopped
2 garlic cloves, finely chopped
1 red chilli, seeded and finely chopped
1 tbsp chopped fresh sage
2 x 400g cans chopped tomatoes
400g (14oz) cans haricot beans, drained and rinsed
1 tsp smoked paprika
1 tbsp chopped fresh flat-leaf parsley
salt and freshly ground black pepper
crusty bread or mashed potatoes, to serve

METHOD

Preheat the oven to 180°C (350°F), Gas mark 4. Heat one tablespoon of the oil in a large heavy based frying pan. Add the sausages and cook gently for 1-2 minutes, or until just sealed and lightly browned on all sides. Transfer to a plate and set aside until needed.

Wipe out the frying pan and then add the remaining three tablespoons of the olive oil. Tip in the onion, celery, garlic, chilli and sage, then sauté very gently for about 10 minutes, until the onion is completely softened but not coloured, stirring occasionally. Add the tomatoes and bring to a simmer, then cook for about 10 minutes, until the sauce is slightly reduced and thickened, stirring occasionally. Season to taste.

Transfer the tomato mixture to a small roasting tin or casserole dish that fits the mixture quite snugly and stir in the haricot beans and smoked paprika, then arrange the sausages on top, burying them down into the mixture. Roast for 20-25 until the cassoulet is bubbling and the sausages are cooked through and tender. Scatter the parsley over and serve straight to the table with a bowl of crusty bread or mashed potatoes and allow guests to help themselves.

GRILLED LAMB PITTAS

Try serving these deliciously, succulent lamb burgers with a minted yoghurt dip, made from 200ml (7fl oz) Greek style yoghurt, a quarter cucumber that has been grated with the water squeezed out, a handful shredded mint leaves and a crushed garlic clove. Alternatively using minced chicken or turkey instead of the lamb – both are really lean and low in fat.

INGREDIENTS
SERVES 4

900g (2lb) lean minced lamb
2 tbsp chopped fresh flat-leaf parsley
1 tbsp chopped fresh mint
1 onion, finely chopped
1 garlic clove, crushed
1 egg
1 tbsp sweet chilli sauce
4 wholemeal pitta breads
50g (2oz) wild rocket

FOR THE MINT SALAD:

3 vine ripened tomatoes, sliced
1 red onion, thinly sliced
1 tbsp chopped fresh mint
1 tbsp olive oil
2 tbsp fresh lemon juice
salt and freshly ground black pepper

METHOD

Place the minced lamb in a large bowl with the parsley, mint, onion, garlic, egg and sweet chilli sauce. Mix together until well combined and then divide the mixture into eight equal portions. Using wetted hands, shape into patties and then arrange on a baking sheet. Cover with clingfilm and chill for 30 minutes to allow the mixture to firm up.

Preheat the grill and the oven to 160°C (325°F), Gas mark 3. Arrange the patties on a grill rack and cook for 10 minutes or until cooked through and golden brown, turning once.

Meanwhile, wrap the pitta bread in foil and place in the oven for 5 minutes to warm through. To make mint salad, place the tomatoes, red onion, mint, olive oil and lemon juice in a bowl. Season to taste and toss gently to coat.

To serve, remove the pitta breads from the oven and split open each pocket, then fill with the rocket, some mint salad and the lamb burgers.

SWEET POTATO & CRISPY BACON PASTA

This sweet potato and crispy bacon pasta is the kind of meal I tend to make when I haven't got much time on my hands but want something really tasty. It really is very easy to prepare and an excellent one-pot wonder. Lardons, by the way, are cubes or strips of smoked bacon. This recipe is also good with turkey or chicken.

INGREDIENTS
SERVES 4

2 sweet potatoes
2 tbsp olive oil
25g (1oz) butter
100g (4oz) piece bacon, rind removed and cut into lardons
2 garlic cloves, crushed
1 red onion, finely diced
175g (6oz) mushrooms, sliced
100ml (3½floz) vegetable stock
250g tub mascarpone cheese
275g (10oz) penne pasta
50g (2oz) toasted pine nuts (optional)
1 tsp chopped fresh basil
salt and freshly ground black pepper
lightly dressed salad and crusty bread, to serve

METHOD

Preheat the oven to 200°C (400°F), Gas mark 6. Peel the sweet potatoes, then cut them into bite-size chunks. Place half of the olive oil and the butter in a roasting tin. Place in the oven for a few minutes to heat up. Then toss the sweet potatoes into the heated oil and butter mixture. Roast for 20 minutes, or until just cooked through. Keep warm.

Heat the remaining olive oil in a frying pan and add the bacon. Cook for 5 minutes, until crisp and lightly golden. Then add garlic, onion and mushrooms and cook for another 5 minutes, until the mushrooms are tender, stirring regularly.

Stir in the stock, mascarpone cheese and simmer very gently for 5 minutes, until slightly reduced and thickened. Season to taste.

Meanwhile, cook the penne pasta in a large pan of boiling, salted water for 8 to 10 minutes, until al dente (tender but still firm to the bite), or according to packet instructions. Drain and then quickly refresh under cold running water. Return to the pan and stir in the mascarpone sauce. Then carefully fold in the roasted sweet potatoes and pine nuts, if using. Divide among warmed bowls and scatter over the basil. Serve at once with a separate bowl of salad and some crusty bread.

SIZZLING CHICKEN FAJITAS WITH TOMATO SALSA

Kids just seem to love this dish and luckily it's actually very good for them and full of protein. I always keep a packet of flour tortillas in the cupboard as they often come in handy.

INGREDIENTS
SERVES 4

3 tbsp sunflower oil
1 red onion, thinly sliced
1 red pepper, cored, seeded and cut into thin strips
4 skinless chicken breast fillets, cut into strips
25g packet fajita seasoning mix
8 soft flour tortillas (1 packet)
1 bunch spring onions, trimmed and thinly sliced

FOR THE TOMATO SALSA:

1 tbsp olive oil
1 small onion, roughly chopped
1 garlic clove, crushed
400g can chopped tomatoes
pinch of sugar
pinch of hot chilli powder
3 tbsp chopped fresh coriander
salt and freshly ground black pepper
soured cream and lime wedges, to serve

METHOD

First make the tomato salsa. Heat the olive oil in a pan and gently fry the onion and garlic for 3-4 minutes, until softened but not coloured, stirring occasionally. Add the tomatoes, sugar and chilli powder. Bring to a simmer, then cook for 15 minutes until reduced and slightly thickened. Transfer to a serving bowl, stir in the coriander and season to taste.

To make the fajitas, heat two tablespoons of oil in a large frying pan and gently fry the red onion and red pepper for 6-8 minutes over a low heat, until softened, stirring occasionally. Remove with a slotted spoon to a bowl.

Increase the heat and add the remaining oil to the pan. Add the chicken, then sprinkle over the fajita seasoning, stirring to combine. Sauté for 6-8 minutes until cooked though and lightly golden, tossing occasionally. Return the onion and pepper mixture to the pan. Sauté for another 2-3 minutes, until well combined and heated through. Season to taste.

Meanwhile, heat a frying or griddle pan. Add a soft flour tortilla and heat for 30 seconds, turning once until soft and pliable. Repeat with the remaining tortillas and stack them up on a warmed plate.

Transfer the spicy chicken mixture and tomato salsa into bowls and put with the heated tortillas on the centre of the table, then have separate bowls of the spring onions, soured cream and lime wedges. Allow each person to assemble the fajitas themselves, so have plenty of napkins to hand.

I just never seem to be able to make enough of these. Fortunately, they take just minutes to make and seconds to demolish. You have been warned! Don't forget to hand around a separate dish for used cocktail sticks. If you wish, you can leave the sausages to marinate for a few hours in the fridge, and this will improve the flavour greatly.

INGREDIENTS
SERVES 4-6

20 cocktail sausages, about 350g (12oz) in total
2 tbsp hoisin or sweet chilli sauce
2 tsp dark soy sauce
2 tsp runny honey
1 tbsp sesame seeds

METHOD

Preheat the oven to 200°C (400°F), Gas mark 6. Place the sausages in a single layer in a non-stick roasting tin. Mix together the hoisin or sweet chilli sauce, soy sauce and honey in a bowl and pour over the sausages, turning to coat.

Bake the sausages for 20 minutes, then drain off any excess fat and sprinkle over the sesame seeds. Cook for another 15 minutes or until golden and sticky. To serve, arrange on a warmed plate skewered with cocktail sticks.

SHEPHERD'S PIE

This recipe can be prepared a day in advance or made up and frozen until needed. It also works very well with minced beef although my personal favourite is with lamb.

INGREDIENTS
SERVES 4

1 tbsp olive oil
450g (1lb) lean minced lamb
2 smoked bacon rashers, rind removed and diced
1 onion, chopped
4 carrots, diced
1 garlic clove, crushed
2 tbsp Worcestershire sauce
300ml (½ pint) lamb or beef stock
1 tbsp tomato purée
1 teaspoon chopped fresh thyme
1 tbsp chopped fresh parsley
100g (4oz) frozen garden peas, thawed

FOR THE CHEESY MASH:

900g (2lb) floury potatoes, cut into cubes
25g (1oz) butter
100ml (3 ½fl oz) milk
50g (2oz) mature Cheddar cheese, grated

METHOD

Heat a large saucepan and add the oil. Tip in the mince and smoked bacon and sauté for about 5 minutes until browned all over, breaking up any lumps with a wooden spoon. Remove from the pan with a slotted spoon and set aside. Cook the onion, carrots and garlic and cook for 4-5 minutes stirring until just changing colour.

Stir the Worcestershire sauce into the vegetable mixture with the reserved mince, then add stock, tomato purée and thyme. Mix well to combine, then cover and simmer for 20 minutes, until the mince is completely tender and cooked through. Finally, stir in the parsley and peas and season to taste.

Place cooked mince into an ovenproof dish. Leave to cool slightly for about 20 minutes.

Preheat the oven to 180°C (350°F), Gas mark 4.

Meanwhile, gently steam the potatoes until tender. Mash well, making sure there are no lumps. Beat in milk, butter and Cheddar cheese, and season to taste. Gently spoon the cheesy mash on top of mince, spreading it with a fork in an even manner.

Place the shepherd's pie in the oven for 15-20 minutes until the cheesy mash is golden brown. Serve straight to the table for all the family to enjoy.

Fish And Seafood

HERB AND NUT CRUSTED COD FILLETS

This is a very versatile crust, and you could use it on monkfish, haddock, organic salmon, or even wild salmon. I always insist on buying cod with the skin on. For this recipe it helps keep the fish together. And you know it is cod you are buying when you can see the skin!

INGREDIENTS
SERVES 6

150g (5oz) wholemeal bread
50g (2oz) shelled walnuts, roughly chopped
3 tbsp chopped fresh flat-leaf parsley
3 tbsp snipped chives
finely grated rind of 1 orange
pinch of freshly grated nutmeg
75g (3oz) butter
6 x 175g (6oz) cod fillets, skin on with pin bones removed
1 egg yolk, beaten

FOR THE LEMON BUTTER SAUCE:

½ small onion, diced
juice and grated rind of 1 large lemon
100ml (3 ½fl oz) dry white wine
150ml (¼ pint) cream
1 tsp Dijon mustard
50g (2oz) butter
1 tsp snipped fresh chives
salt and freshly ground black pepper
steamed new potatoes and fine green beans, to serve

METHOD

Preheat the oven 200°C (400°F), Gas mark 6. Whizz the bread in the food processor to make crumbs. Mix in a bowl with the walnuts, herbs, orange rind and nutmeg.

Heat the butter in a saucepan until just melted. Stir into the crumb mixture. Mix well and allow to cool. Place the cod skin-side down on a non-stick baking sheet and rub the flesh with salt and pepper. Brush the top of the cod with the beaten egg yolk, and press the crumbs on top to stick. Bake for 15-20 minutes until the fish is firm and the crumbs are crisp.

Meanwhile, make the lemon butter sauce. Place the onion, lemon rind and wine in a medium pan and reduce by half. Whisk in the cream and bring slowly to the boil. Reduce the liquid again by half and then whisk in the lemon juice, mustard and butter. Season to taste and stir in chives just before serving. Serve the cod fillets on warmed plates with a spoonful of the lemon butter sauce and arrange some new potatoes and green beans to the side.

SPAGHETTI WITH PRAWNS

Spaghetti is popular throughout the year. This is a simple white wine cream sauce for any pasta dish. You could also use mussels, natural smoked haddock, or, if you want to push the boat out, lobster, which I enjoyed a while back in Rome.

INGREDIENTS
SERVES 4-6

350g (12oz) spaghetti
150ml (¼ pint) dry white wine
2 garlic cloves, crushed
1 red chilli, seeded and finely chopped
300ml (½ pint) cream
450g (1lb) cooked peeled tiger prawns
1 tbsp shredded fresh basil
1 tbsp chopped fresh flat-leaf parsley
a little extra-virgin olive oil
salt and freshly ground black pepper
lemon wedges, to garnish
crusty bread, to serve

METHOD

Cook the spaghetti in a large saucepan of boiling, salted water for 8 to 10 minutes, or as per packet instructions, until al dente (tender but still firm to the bite).

Meanwhile, pour the wine into a separate large saucepan and add the garlic, chilli and cream. Bring to the boil, then reduce the heat and simmer for 5 minutes, stirring occasionally.

Drain the pasta and tip into the pan of sauce, then add the tiger prawns, basil and parsley. Stir gently until well combined, and season to taste.

To serve, divide the spaghetti with the prawns, among warmed bowls, and drizzle a little olive oil over each one. Garnish with lemon wedges and serve with a separate bowl of crusty bread.

TROUT AND BABY SPINACH LINGUINE

We are lucky in Blacklion to get wild brown trout from the Cladagh Glen. The flavour is exceptional. It is a sweet and succulent fish, and I am sure people have their own good sources around the country. I always think trout is underused, and several varieties are very readily available, some farmed and some wild. You can also use salmon with this recipe.

INGREDIENTS
SERVES 4

400g (14oz) linguine pasta
4 x 75-100g (3-4oz) trout fillets, skinned and boned
2 tsp olive oil
1 tbsp fresh lime juice
50g (2oz) tender baby spinach leaves
6 spring onions, trimmed and finely sliced
1 tbsp chopped fresh dill

FOR THE DRESSING:

100ml (3 ½fl oz) extra-virgin olive oil
1 tbsp fresh lemon juice
100ml (3 ½fl oz) freshly squeezed orange juice
1 tsp Dijon mustard
1 tsp snipped fresh chives
1 tbsp finely diced red onion
salt and freshly ground black pepper
crusty bread, to serve

METHOD

Preheat the grill to high. To make the dressing, place the olive oil in a small bowl with the lemon juice, orange juice, mustard, chives and onion. Whisk together until emulsified and then season to taste.

Plunge the linguine into a large pan of boiling salted water, stir once and cook for 8-10 minutes until just tender – 'al dente'.

Lightly brush trout with the olive oil, season all over and arrange on the grill rack, then cook for 6-8 minutes, turning once and sprinkling over the lime juice half way through cooking.

Place the spinach in a bowl and add the spring onions, dill and dressing. Gently toss to combine, then set aside and allow the flavours to combine.

Drain the linguine and fold in the spinach mixture, then divide among warmed serving plates and arrange the trout fillets on top. Drizzle over the remaining dressing. Hand around the crusty bread at the table.

SEAFOOD PAELLA

Most supermarkets and fishmongers now stock packets of mixed seafood that are perfect to use in this dish; otherwise make up your own selection using what's available.

INGREDIENTS
SERVES 6-8)

100ml (3 ½fl oz) olive oil
8 chicken thighs
150g (5oz) smoked bacon
1 onion, chopped
1 red pepper, cored, seeded and sliced
2 garlic cloves, crushed
4 tomatoes, roughly chopped
200g (7oz) long grain rice
1 tsp paprika
150ml (¼ pint) dry white wine
450ml (3/4 pint) chicken stock
1 tsp saffron strands
1 tbsp chopped fresh thyme
25g (1oz) butter
900g (2lb) mussels, cleaned
450g packet mixed seafood (including squid and prawns)
salt and freshly ground black pepper
crusty bread, to serve

METHOD

Heat half of the oil in a large sauté pan with a lid. Add the chicken thighs and fry for 5 minutes until golden, turning regularly. Add the bacon and sauté for another 5 minutes until the bacon is just cooked through and remove the chicken and bacon from the pan, using a slotted spoon and drain on kitchen paper. Set aside.

Heat the remaining oil in the pan. Add the onion, red pepper, garlic and tomatoes and sauté for 5 minutes until softened. Stir in the rice and paprika and cook for 1 minute until well coated. Mix half the wine in a jug with the stock and saffron, then pour into the pan. Return chicken and bacon to the pan with the thyme. Bring to the boil, then reduce heat, cover and simmer for 15-20 minutes until the rice and chicken are tender and all the liquid has been absorbed.

Meanwhile, melt the butter in a large pan with a lid. Add the mussels and remaining wine. Bring to the boil, then cover and simmer for 3-4 minutes, shaking the pan halfway through. All the mussels should now have opened – discard any that do not. Fold the mixed seafood into the pan until heated through. Add the mussels and a little of their cooking juices – just be careful not to make the paella too soupy. Season to taste and place directly on the table. Serve with a basket of crusty bread.

This way of cooking fish retains the goodness and keeps the fish moist. Fish has become expensive, and for this recipe you could substitute haddock or salmon for the hake, which are good value but cod is great to introduce children to fish.

INGREDIENTS
SERVES 4

3 small carrots, halved
6 tbsp olive oil
2 garlic cloves, crushed
1 red chilli, seeded and finely chopped
1 tsp fresh thyme leaves
3 small parsnips, halved
12 large shallots, peeled and trimmed
1 small butternut squash, peeled, seeded and cut into quarters
50g (2oz) butter
8 fresh bay leaves
3 tbsp chopped fresh flat-leaf parsley
2 pared long strips lime rind
1 tsp coarse ground black pepper
4 x 175g (6oz) haddock fillets, pin bones removed
Maldon salt and freshly ground black pepper

METHOD

Preheat the oven to 190°C (375°F) Gas mark 5. Place the carrots in a pan of boiling water and blanch for 2-3 minutes, then refresh under cold running water to retain their colour. Place four tablespoons of the olive oil in a roasting tin and add the garlic, chilli and thyme. Add all of the vegetables, including the carrots and toss well to combine. Season generously and bake for 40-45 minutes or until the vegetables are until completely tender and lightly caramelised, tossing from time to time to ensure they cook evenly.

About 5 minutes before the vegetables are ready, heat the remaining oil and the butter in a large frying pan. Add the bay leaves, parsley, lime rind and pepper and cook for 2 minutes, stirring. Add the hake and cook for 2-3 minutes on each side or until just cooked through and tender. Arrange the roasted vegetables on warmed plates and top with the hake fillets, then spoon over the pan juices to serve.

ROAST MONKFISH ON A LEEK AND BACON MASH

Monkfish is a round fish that has become hugely popular in Ireland over the last five years or so. Believe it or not, fishermen used to throw it back into the sea. Let's just say it would not win any beauty contests. I find that people who normally won't eat fish enjoy this one. It's very white and has quite a chewy texture, which appeals to meat eaters. See if you can convert a meat eater to fish in your house with this recipe.

INGREDIENTS
SERVES 4

675g (1 ½lb) potatoes, cut into chunks
2 tbsp olive oil
100g (4oz) streaky bacon rashers, rinds removed and diced
75g (3oz) butter
75g (3oz) leeks, trimmed and sliced
120ml (4fl oz) red wine
250ml (9fl oz) beef stock
1 tsp caster sugar
1 tsp balsamic vinegar
1 tsp tomato purée
1 fresh thyme sprig
4 x 150g (5oz) monkfish tails, well trimmed
salt and freshly ground black pepper
chopped fresh flat-leaf parsley, to garnish

METHOD

Preheat the oven to 230°C (450°F), Gas mark 8. Cook the potatoes in a saucepan of boiling salted water for 15-20 minutes until tender. Drain and return to the pan to dry out a little. Mash well and keep warm.

Meanwhile, heat half the oil in a pan and cook the bacon until just crispy and lightly browned, remove to a dish. Add 50g (2oz) of the butter to this pan and sweat the leeks in it for 2 minutes or until just cooked and soft. Mix the crispy bacon and buttered leek mixture into the mashed potatoes. Season to taste, being careful not to over salt with the bacon in the mash Keep warm.

To make the sauce, heat the wine in a saucepan and reduce by half. Add the stock and reduce slightly again. Add the sugar, vinegar and purée, then cook for 2 minutes, stirring. Add the thyme and keep warm.

To prepare the fish, heat the rest of the butter and oil in an ovenproof pan until foaming. Add the monkfish tails to the pan, presentation-side down and cook for a minute or two until golden brown. Turn over and cook for another 2 minutes until golden. Season and place the pan in the oven for about 3 minutes or until the monkfish is just cooked through and tender.

To serve, spoon some leek and bacon mash into the centre of warmed plates, put the monkfish on top and drizzle the red wine sauce around the edges of the plates. Garnish with some parsley to serve.

TUNA NIÇOISE

The tuna for this classic salad is cooked medium rare so that it remains moist, but cook it for a minute or two longer if you prefer, or use canned tuna.

INGREDIENTS
SERVES 4

100g (4oz) fresh tuna steaks, each about 2.5cm (1in) thick
12 new salad potatoes
4 eggs, at room temperature
100g (4oz) extra-fine French beans, trimmed
4 little Gem lettuce hearts, quartered lengthways and separated into leaves
4 ripe plum tomatoes, roughly chopped
½ small red onion, thinly sliced
6 anchovy fillets, drained and cut lengthways into thin strips
16 pitted black olives in brine, drained
8 fresh basil leaves, torn

FOR THE MARINADE:

7 tbsp extra-virgin olive oil
3 tbsp aged red wine vinegar
2 tbsp chopped fresh flat-leaf parsley
2 tbsp snipped fresh chives
2 garlic cloves, finely chopped
salt and freshly ground black pepper

METHOD

To make marinade, place the olive oil, vinegar, parsley, chives, garlic and a teaspoon each of salt and pepper in a bowl and whisk to combine.

Place the tuna in a shallow, non-metallic dish and pour over half of the marinade. Cover with clingfilm and chill for 1–2 hours to allow the flavours to penetrate the tuna, turning every 30 minutes or so. Place the potatoes in a pan of boiling salted water, cover and simmer for 15–18 minutes until just tender. Drain and leave to cool completely, then cut lengthways into quarters.

Place the eggs in a small pan and just cover with boiling water, then cook for 6 minutes. Drain and rinse under cold running water, then remove the shells and cut each egg in half. Plunge the French beans in a pan of boiling salted water and blanch for a minute or so, then drain and refresh under cold running water.

Heat a griddle pan for 5 minutes until very hot. Remove the tuna from the marinade, shaking off any excess. Cook the tuna steaks for 2–3 minutes on each side. Arrange the lettuce leaves on plates or one large platter and add the potatoes, French beans, tomatoes, onion and anchovies. Place the tuna steaks on top and drizzle over the remaining marinade. Decorate with the egg halves, olives and torn basil leaves.

PAN-FRIED MACKEREL WITH TOMATO STEW AND BASIL PESTO

Nowadays, you'll often hear people on radio and television talking about "good fats" and "bad fats". We are urged to eat more oily fish to increase our intake of "good fats". Well, let me tell you that mackerel is one of the best examples of a good, oily fish. As well as this important health factor, mackerel is also great value for money, has a lovely meaty texture and is definitely under used. It is delicious grilled with a simple salad. The secret with mackerel is always to cook it as fresh as you can get it. The tomato and pesto are also great sauces with pasta and very popular with children.

INGREDIENTS
SERVES 4

1 tbsp olive oil
1 onion, sliced
1 garlic clove, crushed
4 vine ripened tomatoes, cut into chunks
dash of red wine vinegar
1 tsp sugar
1 tsp tomato purée
4 mackerel fillets

FOR THE BASIL PESTO:

2 bunches fresh basil, leaves stripped
75g (3oz) freshly grated Parmesan cheese
50g (2oz) toasted pine nuts
2 garlic cloves
250ml (9fl oz) olive oil
salt and freshly ground black pepper

METHOD

First make the basil pesto by putting the basil leaves, Parmesan, pine nuts and garlic in a blender. Blend until well chopped up and season to taste. Add the olive oil and blend again until smooth. Keep in a jar or a squeeze bottle in the fridge.

Heat one tablespoon of oil in a saucepan and add the onion and garlic, then cook gently for 1-2 minutes. Add the tomatoes, vinegar, sugar and tomato purée. Stir well and season to taste. Leave this sauce cook out slowly until the mixture dries out a little, about 5 minutes should do it.

Preheat a heavy-based griddle pan. Score the skin of the mackerel three times on each side and add to the griddle pan, skin-side down. Cook for 2 minutes, then turn over and cook for a further 2 minutes or until the mackerel fillets are cooked through and tender. To serve, place the mackerel in the centre of each warmed plate and spoon some stewed tomatoes alongside. Drizzle with basil pesto around the edges of the plates to serve.

SALMON AND SPINACH EN CROUTE

These salmon and spinach croutes are perfect for serving at a dinner party. Make sure you get the best organic farmed salmon, as there really is a quality difference. Or you can use sea trout, which is good value.

INGREDIENTS
SERVES 4

100g (4oz) unsalted butter, softened
1 tbsp chopped fresh tarragon
2 tbsp chopped fresh flat-leaf parsley
1 tbsp chopped fresh dill
1 garlic clove, crushed
500g packet puff pastry, thawed if frozen
a little plain flour, for dusting
4 x 175g (6oz) salmon fillets, skinned and boned (about 2.5cm (1in) thick)
50g (2oz) baby spinach leaves
1 egg, beaten
salt and freshly ground black pepper
lightly dressed green salad, to serve

METHOD

Preheat the oven to 200°C (400°F). Gas mark 6. Place the butter in a small bowl and beat in the tarragon with the parsley, dill and garlic and season generously.

Spoon on to a sheet of clingfilm or parchment paper and shape into a roll about is 2.5cm (1in) thick, then wrap tightly. Chill in the freezer for at least 10 minutes to firm up (or keep in the fridge for up to 48 hours, until required, if time allows).

Cut the pastry into eight even-sized sections and roll each one out on a lightly floured surface to a 12.5-18cm (5 x 7in) rectangle, trimming down the edges as necessary. Arrange four of the rectangles on baking sheets lined with parchment paper. Place a salmon fillet in the centre of each one. Unwrap the garlic butter, cut into thin slices and arrange in an overlapping layer on each piece of salmon. Cover with the spinach leaves and season to taste.

Brush the edges of the pastry bases with a little of the beaten egg and lay a second sheet of pastry on top, pressing down to seal. Crimp the edges by gently pressing the edge of the pastry with the forefinger of one hand and between the first two fingers of the other hand. Continue all the way around the edge of the parcel, then repeat until you have four parcels in total. Using a sharp knife, make light slashes across the top of each parcel, being careful not to cut right through.

Brush the pastry parcels with the remaining beaten egg and bake for 25-30 minutes, or until the pastry is cooked through and golden brown. Arrange the salmon parcels on warmed serving plates with some salad to serve.

MACNEAN FISH PIE

Fish pie is a real staple of Irish family cooking and everyone has their own way of making it. This is my version which everyone always seems to enjoy.

INGREDIENTS
SERVES 6-8

350g (12oz) each haddock, smoked cod and salmon fillets, skin on and bones removed
1 large bay leaf
900ml (1 ½ pints) milk
800g (1lb 12oz) floury potatoes, cut into cubes
2 tbsp basil pesto (see recipie p.126)
50g (2oz) butter
225g (8oz) leeks, thinly sliced
1 small onion, thinly sliced
50g (2oz) plain flour
150ml (¼ pint) dry white wine
1 tbsp chopped fresh mixed herbs (use parsley, chives and dill)
150g (5oz) cooked peeled prawns
2 tbsp crème fraîche
2 heaped tbsp toasted breadcrumbs
salt and freshly ground white pepper
steamed broccoli florets, to serve

METHOD

Preheat the oven to 160°C (325°F), Gas mark 3. Season the haddock, cod and salmon and place in a roasting tin with the bay leaf and milk. Poach in the oven for 10-15 minutes or until the fish flakes easily when tested with a knife. Remove the fish from the tin and take off the skin. Flake the flesh, checking for bones that might have been overlooked. Strain the leftover milk into a measuring jug until you have 600ml (1 pint). Discard the bay leaf. Increase the temperature of the oven to 180°C (350°F), Gas mark 4.

Place the potatoes in a large pan of salted water, bring to the boil and cook for 15 minutes or until tender. Drain and return to the pan to dry out a little. Mash well and beat in half of the butter and half of the pesto. Season well.

Melt the remaining butter in a small pan and gently cook the leeks and onion for about 5 minutes. Stir in the flour and cook for 1 minute, stirring constantly. Pour in the white wine and reduce by half. Gradually pour in the reserved poaching milk and stir until you have a smooth sauce. Season and reduce the heat. Add the herbs and simmer for 3 minutes, stirring occasionally. Lastly add the prawns, flaked fish and crème fraîche and cook for 2 minutes. Be careful not to boil the mixture because the fish will break up and the sauce will go mushy.

Spoon the fish mixture into a shallow ovenproof dish and dot with the remaining pesto. Top it with the flavoured mash and sprinkle over breadcrumbs. Bake for about 20 minutes or until the top is golden. To serve, divide among warmed plates and add some broccoli to each one.

SMOKED SALMON AND RED ONION QUICHE

Amelda loves smoked salmon, so I often do this quiche. You can make this a day ahead. It is even better the next day. Just chill it overnight and gently warm in the oven for about 20 minutes. Very tasty.

INGREDIENTS
SERVES 4-6

150ml (¼ pint) cream
150ml (¼ pint) milk
2 tbsp sweet chilli sauce
2 eggs, plus 2 egg yolks plus a little egg wash, for brushing
1 tbsp snipped fresh chives
200g (7oz) smoked salmon, cut into strips
1 red onion, finely diced
100g (4 oz) freshly grated Parmesan cheese

FOR THE PASTRY:

225g (8oz) plain flour, plus extra for dusting
100g (4oz) chilled butter, diced
pinch of dried chilli flakes
3 tbsp ice-cold water
salt and freshly ground black pepper
crisp garden salad, to serve

METHOD

Preheat oven to 200°C (400°F), Gas mark 6. To make the pastry, place the flour, butter and chilli flakes in a food processor. Add half a teaspoon of salt and whizz briefly until the mixture forms fine crumbs. Pour in the water through the feeder tube and pulse until the pastry comes together. Knead lightly on a lightly floured surface for a few seconds to give a smooth dough. Wrap in clingfim and chill for at least 10 minutes (or up to an hour if time allows).

Roll out the pastry on a lightly floured surface and use to line a loose-bottomed 21cm (8 ½in) fluted flan tin that is about 4cm (1 ½in) deep. Use a rolling pin to lift the pastry into the tin, pressing well into sides and letting the pastry overhang a little as this prevents shrinkage. Chill for 10 minutes.

Prick the pastry base with a fork, then line with a circle of foil or parchment paper that is first crumpled up to make it easier to handle. Fill with baking beans or dried pulses and bake blind for 10 minutes until the pastry case looks 'set', but not coloured. Carefully remove the foil or paper and lower the oven temperature to 160°C (325°F), Gas mark 3, then brush with the egg wash to form a seal. Return to the oven for another 5 minutes until lightly coloured.

Beat the cream in a bowl with the milk, chilli sauce, eggs and egg yolks. Stir in the chives and season to taste. Scatter the smoked salmon in the pastry case and sprinkle the red onion and Parmesan on top, then pour in the cream mixture and bake for about 25 minutes until just set but still slightly wobbly in the middle. Remove and trim down the excess pastry. To serve, cut the tart into slices and arrange on plates with the salad.

Desserts

SUMMER BERRY MERINGUE ROULADE

There's something delightfully decadent about summer desserts. The combination of bright berry colours, squishy meringue and softly whipped cream just makes my mouth water.

INGREDIENTS
SERVES ABOUT 8

5 large egg whites
300g (11oz) caster sugar
1 tsp white wine vinegar
2 tsp cornflour
1 tsp vanilla extract
350ml (12fl oz) cream
350g (12oz) mixed summer berries, (such as a mixture of halved small strawberries, raspberries, blackberries and blueberries)
fresh mint leaves, to decorate

METHOD

Preheat the oven to 150°C (300°F), Gas mark 2. Lightly grease a Swiss roll tin and line with parchment paper. First, make the meringue. In a large clean bowl, whisk the egg whites to form stiff peaks. While still beating, gradually add the sugar bit by bit to give a stiff and glossy mixture. Add the vinegar, cornflour and vanilla extract and fold in gently.

Spread the meringue mixture out evenly into the prepared tin and bake for 20 minutes before reducing the temperature to 110°C (230°F), Gas mark ½. Cook for another 25-30 minutes, until cooked through and springy to touch.

Remove meringue roulade from the oven and leave in the tin for 15 minutes to cool a little. Lay a large piece of parchment paper, just bigger than the roulade, out on a surface.

Carefully tip the meringue roulade top-side down onto the paper and peel off the paper lightly stuck to the bottom. Leave to cool completely. Softly whip the cream and spread it over the cooled roulade. Scatter almost all of the fruit over the top, reserving some for decoration. Starting at one short edge, use the parchment paper to gently lift and roll the roulade away from you until you get to the end.

Carefully transfer the meringue roulade to sit seam side-down on a large serving platter. Scatter over the reserved berries and decorate with fresh mint sprigs. Serve straight to the table and cut into slices to serve on individual plates.

NUTELLA CHEESECAKE

This decedent cheesecake is fabulously smooth, silky and rich. It is perfect if you want to make something the day before and keep it in the fridge until needed. If you want to increase the chocolate hit try using chocolate ginger nut biscuits for the base!

INGREDIENTS
SERVES 6-8

FOR THE BASE:

75g (3oz) butter, plus extra for greasing
250g (9oz) ginger nut biscuits, crushed

FOR THE FILLING:

1 vanilla pod, split in half and seeds removed
2 x 250g tubs mascarpone cheese
100g (4oz) caster sugar
2 tbsp cornflour
3 eggs
200g jar Nutella (chocolate and hazelnut spread)
mini chocolate Easter eggs, to decorate (optional)
icing sugar, to dust
whipped cream, to serve

METHOD

Preheat oven to 160°C (325°F), Gas mark 3. To make the base, lightly butter a 23cm (9in) spring-form cake tin. Melt the butter in a pan over a gentle heat or in a bowl in the microwave. Add the crushed ginger nut biscuits and mix well. Spread the mixture evenly over the base of the tin, pressing down with the back of a spoon to flatten. Place in fridge to chill for 15 minutes.

Place a dish or baking tin of hot water in oven on the bottom rack; this will stop a skin forming on the cheesecake. Using the paddle attachment on a food processor, place the vanilla seeds, mascarpone cheese, sugar, cornflour, eggs and Nutella in the mixing bowl. Beat until smooth.

Pour this nutella mixture onto the biscuit base in the cake tin and place on a baking sheet.

Bake for 50-55 minutes until just set around the edges but still be a little wobbly in the centre. Turn off the oven, open the door and carefully run a knife around the cake tin, this prevents the cheesecake from splitting in the middle when cooling. Close the oven door and leave for 1 ½ hours until completely set. Remove from the oven and place in the fridge if not using immediately.

To serve, transfer the cheesecake to a cake stand and decorate with the mini chocolate eggs, if liked, then dust lightly with icing sugar and cut into wedges in front of your guests. Add a dollop of whipped cream to each plate to serve.

VANILLA CRÈME BRÛLÉE WITH PLUM COMPOTE

Alternatively, place the brûlées under a hot grill, but watch them like a hawk because they do burn very easily. When glazed they should be a nice mahogany brown colour but don't go poking your fingers into the brûlée topping as the hot sugar will burn! Ouch!

INGREDIENTS
SERVES 8

8 egg yolks
250g (9oz) caster sugar
1 vanilla pod, split in half and seeds scraped out
300ml (½ pint) milk
600ml (1 pint) cream
400g can coconut milk

FOR THE PLUM COMPOTE:

150ml (¼ pint) red wine
175g (6oz) caster sugar
1 cinnamon stick
1 star anise
1 vanilla pod, split in half and seeds scraped out
450g (1lb) ripe plums, halved, stoned and cut into slices

METHOD

Preheat oven to 90°C (185°F), Gas mark ¼. Place the egg yolks in a large bowl with 125g (4 ½oz) of the sugar and the scraped out vanilla seeds. Beat together lightly.

Meanwhile, place the milk in a pan with the cream, coconut milk and scraped out vanilla pod and then simmer gently until the mixture just comes to the boil. Slowly pour the hot coconut milk mixture into the yolk mixture, disregarding the vanilla pod and whisking continuously. Pass through a sieve into a clean bowl.

Using a ladle, divide the mixture into 8 x 200ml (7fl oz) ramekins that are arranged in a roasting tin and cover the whole tin tightly with foil. Bake in the oven for 50-55 minutes or until just set but still with a slight wobble in the middle, remove from the oven and leave to cool still covered in the foil for 30 minutes. Remove the foil and allow to cool completely. Transfer to the fridge and allow to set for at least 6 hours, or preferably overnight.

Meanwhile, poach the plums. Place the wine in a pan with 150ml (¼ pint) of water, the sugar, cinnamon, star anise and vanilla seeds. Slowly bring to the boil, then reduce the heat and simmer gently for 20-25 minutes until reduced by half and syrupy in texture. Add the plums to the wine mixture and simmer gently for another 2 minutes until softened but still holding their shape, stirring occasionally but being careful not to damage the plums. Remove from the heat and leave to cool completely.

To serve, sprinkle each of the brûlées in an even layer with the remaining caster sugar and then use a blowtorch to melt and glaze the sugar until golden brown and caramelised or you can use a very hot grill. Arrange on plates and spoon on the poached plums.

APPLE AND BLACKBERRY CRUMBLE

A classic combination of autumn fruit with a crumble topping. I just love making this in autumn when there are still plenty of blackberries around. The crumble mixture really works well on top of any fruit and the soft brown sugar gives the crumble its famous crunchiness. To make a large one simply cook for 45-50 minutes depending on the size of the dish.

INGREDIENTS

SERVES 4-6

300ml (½ pint) apple juice
450g (1lb) Bramley apples, peeled, cored and sliced
100g (4oz) blackberries

FOR THE CRUMBLE:

175g (6oz) plain flour
100g (4oz) butter, at room temperature
100g (4oz) soft brown sugar
1 tsp ground cinnamon
50g (2oz) shelled walnuts, finely chopped

FOR THE CITRUS CREAM:

250g (9oz) tub mascarpone cheese
finely grated rind of 1 orange
1 lemon and 1 lime
½ vanilla pod, split in half and seeds scraped out
1-2 tbsp sifted icing sugar

METHOD

Preheat the oven to 180°C (350°F), Gas mark 4. To make the filling, bring the apple juice to the boil in a saucepan. Add the apples and bring to just before boiling point before removing apples using a slotted spoon. Place in a bowl, then add the blackberries and leave to cool.

To make the crumble, place the flour in a bowl and rub in the butter until the mixture resembles fine breadcrumbs. Stir in the sugar, cinnamon and walnuts until well combined.

Spoon the filling mixture into four to six individual ovenproof dishes or large ramekins. Sprinkle over the crumble mixture and arrange on a baking sheet, then bake for about 20 minutes until the crumble topping is golden brown and bubbling around the edges.

Meanwhile, make the citrus cream, place the mascarpone cheese in a bowl and beat

in the citrus rinds with the vanilla seeds and enough icing sugar to taste. Chill until needed.

To serve, make quenelles of the citrus cream and use to top each apple and blackberry crumble.

PASSION FRUIT CURD PAVLOVA WITH RASPBERRY COULIS

This recipe will produce a meringue that is crunchy on the outside, yet slightly soft in the middle, and I promise you it is pure delicious. I visited Pat Clarke, the most fantastic Bord Bia accredited grower while filming my last series for the TV. The flavour of his berries were absolutely amazing! So it's worth checking on the label where the berries that you buy have been grown.

INGREDIENTS
SERVES 6

4 egg whites
1 vanilla pod, split in half and seeds scraped out
225g (8oz) caster sugar
200g (7oz) fresh raspberries and/or strawberries
50g (2oz) white chocolate, finely grated

FOR THE PASSION FRUIT CURD:

2 eggs plus 2 egg yolks
100g (4oz) caster sugar
finely grated rind of 1 lemon and the juice of 2 lemons
4 passion fruit, halved and pulp scooped out
100g (4 oz) unsalted butter
100 ml (3 ½fl oz) cream, whipped

FOR THE RASPBERRY COULIS:

25g (1oz) sugar
100g (4oz) fresh raspberries
6 fresh mint sprigs, to decorate

METHOD

Preheat the oven to 110°C (225°F), Gas mark ½. Line a large baking sheet with parchment paper. First, to make the Pavlovas, whisk the egg whites with the vanilla until stiff and then continuing to whisk, gradually adding the sugar. Whisk until thick and glossy and the whites form stiff peaks (and you can turn the bowl upside down, without the mixture falling out). Spoon onto the baking sheet in six individual mounds and make a dip in the centre of each with the back of the spoon. Bake for 1 hour until the bottoms are crisp and sound hollow when tapped. Remove them carefully from the baking sheet to avoid breaking and leave to cool on a wire rack.

Meanwhile, make the passion fruit curd. Place the eggs, egg yolks, sugar, lemon rind and juice and passion fruit pulp into a bowl set over a pan of gently-simmering water and stirring constantly, cook for 15-20 minutes, until thickened enough to coat the back of a spoon. (It is important not to let the water boil, as this could curdle the eggs). Remove and leave to cool for 20 minutes. Whisk in the butter and leave to cool, then whisk in the cream.

To make the coulis, place the sugar in a small saucepan with 25g (1fl oz) water and bring slowly to the boil. Reduce to simmer for 2-3 minutes and then remove and allow to cool. Place in a mini blender, add the raspberries and blitz to a purée. Pass through a sieve set over a bowl to catch the coulis.

To serve, place a pavlova onto each plate. Spoon curd into the centre dip of each one and top with the fresh berries. Drizzle over the coulis and scatter the white chocolate on top, then decorate with the mint sprigs.

CHOCOLATE POTS
WITH SHORTBREAD

These chocolate pots are rich, light and fluffy and just perfect served with shortbread on the side. Good-quality chocolate makes all the difference. Try and get chocolate with a minimum of 50% cocoa solids. Instead of Baileys, some people prefer rum or whiskey.

INGREDIENTS
SERVES 6

450ml (3/4 pint) cream
75g (3oz) caster sugar
1 tsp vanilla extract
250g (9oz) plain chocolate, broken into squares (or buttons)
small pinch salt
3 tbsp baileys Irish cream
1 large egg, beaten

FOR THE SHORTBREAD:

40g (1 ½oz) icing sugar, plus extra for dusting
250g (9oz) butter, at room temperature
50g (2oz) cornflour
175g (6oz) plain flour
1 tsp vanilla extract
pinch salt
whipped cream and grated plain chocolate, to decorate

METHOD

To make the shortbread, sift the icing sugar into a bowl and add the butter, then beat together with an electric beater until just combined. Sift the cornflour and plain flour into a separate bowl. Add the vanilla to the butter mixture and then tip in the flour and cornflour with the salt. Mix to form a smooth dough. Mould and shape into a log, then wrap in clingfilm and chill for at least 30 minutes or overnight is fine.

Preheat the oven to 180°C (350°F), Gas mark 4. Remove the shortbread dough from the fridge and cut into 1cm (½in) slices, then cut into shapes with a 5cm (2in) fluted edge. Re-roll the excess dough and repeat until dough is used up. Place on a baking sheet lined with parchment paper. Bake for 15-20 minutes until golden brown. Leave to cool on wire rack, then dust with icing sugar.

To make the chocolate pots, pour the cream into a small pan and add the sugar and vanilla. Warm gently for 3-4 minutes, stirring occasionally but do not allow to boil. Remove from the heat and stir in chocolate until melted, then whisk in the Baileys with the salt and egg until well combined.

Pour the chocolate mixture into teacups, gently tapping until tops are smooth, cover loosely with clingfilm then leave somewhere cold but not the fridge for 4 hours to set. Alternatively chill overnight and allow to come back to room temperature. To serve, put the teacups on to saucers and arrange the shortbread to the side.

RHUBARB UPSIDE DOWN CAKE

It has been a great summer for rhubarb. I get my rhubarb from my Auntie Kathleen, who lives nearby in Dowra, Co. Leitrim. She is a fantastic gardener, and I also get spinach and chives from her. And she supplies me with her eggs for breakfasts. Up and down the country there are so many like her, who supply great food. This cake is a part of a rhubarb plate I serve in the restaurant, and it is very popular. I think rhubarb is undervalued. My customers love it. At home you could also serve this with warm custard.

INGREDIENTS
SERVES 6

125g (4 1/2oz) butter
175g (6oz) caster sugar
3 eggs
175g (175g) plain flour
pinch salt
1 tsp baking powder
1 tbsp milk
1 tsp vanilla extract

FOR THE RHUBARB:

450g (1lb) rhubarb, trimmed
50g (2oz) butter
50g (2oz) soft brown sugar
finely grated rind of 1 orange
toasted flaked almonds, to decorate
icing sugar, to dust
lightly whipped cream, to serve

METHOD

Preheat oven to 180C, 350F, Gas mark 4. To prepare the rhubarb, cut the rhubarb at an angle, into 5cm (2in) slices. Melt the butter and brown sugar in a large ovenproof pan or dish that is about 23cm (9in) in diameter. Stir in the orange rind and remove from heat. Cover the base of the pan with rhubarb.

To make the cake mixture, using an electric mixer, cream the butter and sugar for about 5 minutes until light and fluffy. Fold in one tablespoon of the flour, then gradually add the eggs, one at a time, while still beating until well combined.

Sift the rest of the flour with the salt and baking powder into a separate bowl. Using a tablespoon, gently fold into the bowl with the egg mixture. Finally fold in the milk and vanilla extract until evenly combined. Spread the cake mixture over rhubarb with a spatula. Bake in the oven for about 30 minutes or until the cake mixture is firm to the touch.

Allow the cake to cool for about 20 minutes in the frying pan. Then invert onto a large, flat plate. Sprinkle with toasted almonds and dust with icing sugar. Serve warm cut into slices on plates with a dollop of the whipped cream to the side.

FRUITY BREAD AND BUTTER PUDDING

An Irish country kitchen classic, that should have a soft set texture with an exquisitely light spicing of nutmeg and vanilla, a few finely chopped prunes and sultanas and a wonderful buttery top. To make it even more delicious try making it with day-old croissants or brioche.

INGREDIENTS
SERVES 4-6

75g (3oz) butter, softened plus extra for greasing
4 eggs
300ml (½ pint) milk
150ml (¼ pint) cream
finely grated rind and juice of 1 lemon
1 vanilla pod, split in half and seeds scraped out
6 tbsp clear honey
250g (9oz) sliced white bread
75g (3oz) ready-to-eat dried prunes, finely chopped
75g (3oz) sultanas
good pinch of freshly grated nutmeg
4 tbsp apricot jam pouring cream or vanilla ice cream, to serve

METHOD

Preheat the oven to 180°C (350°F), Gas mark 4 and lightly butter an ovenproof dish. Beat the eggs, milk and cream together in a large jug. Mix together the lemon rind and juice, vanilla pod seeds and honey in a small bowl and then add to the egg mixture, beating lightly to combine.

Spread the slices of bread with the softened butter and cut off the crusts, then cut into triangles. Scatter half of the prunes and sultanas into the bottom of the buttered dish and arrange a layer of the bread triangles on top. Pour over half of the egg mixture, pressing it down gently, then repeat the layers with the remaining ingredients and sprinkle the nutmeg on top.

Place the dish into a roasting tin and fill with warm water so that it comes three-quarters of the way up the dish. Bake for 35-40 minutes until just set. Heat the apricot jam in a small pan and then brush the top of the pudding.

To serve, cut into slices and arrange on serving plates with pouring cream or ice cream.

APPLE AND ALMOND TART

Most fruits can be used instead of the apples, if you fancy a change. Experiment with plums, apricots, blackberries, peaches or raspberries depending on what is in season.

INGREDIENTS
SERVES 6

100g (4oz) butter
100g (4oz) icing sugar, sifted
25g (1oz) plain flour
100g (4oz) ground almonds
2 eggs, lightly beaten
1 vanilla pod, split in half and seeds
scraped out
large pinch of ground cinnamon
450g (1lb) Bramley apples
juice of ½ lemon
2-3 tbsp apricot jam

FOR THE PASTRY:

150g (5oz) butter, diced
175g (6oz) plain flour, plus extra for
dusting
50g (2oz) caster sugar
1 egg yolk
½ tbsp cream
softly whipped cream and caramel ice
cream, to serve

METHOD

To make the pastry, place the butter in a food processor with the flour and sugar and pulse until just blended. Add the egg yolk and cream and blend again briefly. Wrap with clingfilm and chill for one hour to rest.

To make filling, place 100g (4oz) of the butter and the icing sugar in a large bowl and beat until light and fluffy, using an electric hand beater. Beat in the flour and almonds and then gradually beat in the eggs, scraped out vanilla seeds and cinnamon. Continue to beat for 5 minutes until light and fluffy.

Preheat oven to 190°C (375°F), Gas mark 5. Roll out the pastry on a lightly floured surface and use to line a 23cm (9in) loose-bottomed flan tin. Chill again for 15 minutes to allow the pastry to rest.

Peel the apples and cut into quarters to remove the cores, then cut into thin wedges. Tip into a bowl and toss in the lemon juice to prevent them from browning. Spread the almond filling in the pastry case and carefully arrange the apple slices on top in a fan shape and then gently press the apples down into the filling. Dot with the remaining 25g (1oz) of the butter. Bake the tart for 25-30 minutes until the pastry is cooked through and the apples are golden brown. Remove from the flan tin and transfer to a plate. Melt the apricot jam in a pan or in the microwave and brush over the tart.

To serve, cut the tart into wedges and serve warm or cold on serving plates with a good dollop of whipped cream and a scoop of caramel ice cream.

RICE PUDDING WITH RASPBERRY JAM

In many households it is traditional to add a couple of tablespoons of jam into the heart of this pudding. It can also be baked in a preheated oven at 150°C (300°F), Gas mark 2 for 1 hour until the top is golden with a caramelised crust around the edges. The jam makes five jars in total so you'll have a good supply, as it will keep in a cool dark place unopened for one year. Once you've opened a jar, keep it in the fridge.

INGREDIENTS
SERVES 4

100g (4oz) pudding rice (short-grain)
600ml (1 pint) milk
2 tbsp caster sugar
1 vanilla pod, cut in half and seeds
scraped out

FOR THE RASPBERRY JAM:

1.2kg bag granulated sugar, still in
its packet
900g (2lb) raspberries
juice of 1 lemon

METHOD

Preheat oven to 90°C (185°F), Gas mark ¼. To make the jam, warm the sugar in its packet in the oven for 30 minutes. Place the raspberries in a heavy-based saucepan with 600ml (1 pint) of water. Bring to the boil and simmer gently, until the raspberries are tender.

Add the warm sugar and lemon juice to the raspberry mixture. Stir until the sugar is completely dissolved. Bring to the boil again, and boil rapidly for about 20 minutes.

Remove the jam from the heat. Have a cold saucer ready and test by putting a teaspoonful of jam on the saucer. Leave it to cool in the fridge. If the jam wrinkles when you push it with your finger, that means it is ready.

Spoon off any scum from around the edge of the pan, and allow the jam to stand for 15 minutes before stirring once and pouring into warm, sterilised jars. Cover with a wax disc and seal when hot.

To make the rice pudding, place the rice in a deep-sided pan with the milk, sugar and vanilla seeds. Give it all a good stir and then simmer gently for about 30 minutes until the rice pudding is thick and creamy, stirring occasionally.

Divide the rice pudding among warmed bowls and add a large spoonful of the raspberry jam to each one to serve.

Baking In The Afternoon

SPELL BREAD

There are a number of good reasons to eat spelt bread, it is easier for your body to digest than other grains, if may suit your diet if you are gluten sensitive or have a mild wheat allergy. This recipe has come from Katherine O'Leary, a regular contributor to the Farmer's Journal. If you prefer a plain bread, omit the passata but remember to increase the buttermilk accordingly.

INGREDIENTS
MAKES ONE LOAF

sunflower oil, for greasing
175g (6oz) white spelt flour
175g (6oz) wholegrain spelt flour
25g (1oz) mixed seeds, such as linseed, sunflower, sesame seeds and poppy seeds
1 tsp bread soda
120ml (4fl oz) natural yoghurt
450ml (3/4 pint) buttermilk
6 tbsp tomato passata (Italian sieved tomatoes)

METHOD

Preheat the oven to 180°C (350°F), Gas mark 4 and lightly oil a 450g (1lb) loaf tin. In a large bowl, mix together the white spelt, wholegrain spelt, seeds and bread soda, making sure there are no lumps.

Make a well in the centre of the dry ingredients and add the yogurt, buttermilk and passata. Using a wooden spoon, mix gently and quickly until you have loose dough. Drop into the prepared tin. Bake for 45 minutes in the centre of the oven until the bread has risen and slightly come away from the sides of the tin.

Remove the cooked bread from the oven and leave to settle in the tin for a couple of minutes then tip out on to a wire rack and leave to cool completely. To serve, cut into slices and arrange in a breadbasket or use as required.

BAKEWELL SLICE

Be generous with the raspberries, it makes all the difference to this teatime treat. There's no need to line or grease the baking sheet as the pastry already has enough fat and there's no sugar in it to make it stick. Instead of raspberries, you can use apples, strawberries, blackberries or any fruit in season.

INGREDIENTS
SERVES 8

300g (11oz) ready-made shortcrust pastry, thawed if frozen
a little plain flour
50g (2oz) butter, at room temperature
50g (2oz) caster sugar
1 egg
125g (4 ½oz) ground almonds
few drops vanilla extract
250g (9oz) raspberries
50g (2oz) flaked almonds
1 tbsp sifted icing sugar
whipped cream, to serve

METHOD

Preheat oven to 200°C/400°F/Gas 6. Roll out the pastry into 2 x 27.5 x 7.5cm (11 x 3in) rectangles on a lightly floured board. Place on non-stick baking sheets and prick all over with a fork. Bake for 5 minutes until set but not coloured.

Meanwhile, using an electric mixer, beat the butter and sugar together in a bowl until pale and fluffy. Stir in the egg, ground almonds and vanilla extract to make a stiff paste.

Spread the almond paste on top of the pastry, leaving a border around the edges. Gently press the raspberries on to the paste, scatter over the flaked almonds and sift over the icing sugar. Bake for 20–25 minutes until puffed up and lightly golden. Leave on the baking sheets for a few minutes, then carefully transfer to a wire rack to cool. To serve, cut into slices and arrange on plates to serve.

PEANUT TOFFEE SHORTBREAD

Cut into small squares or bars, this shortbread is always popular. For me, it's the different textures that are the principal appeal – the crunch of the shortbread base with the creamy caramel on top. Peanut toffee shortbread is an ideal treat in the school lunch box, and I would much prefer seeing children eating homemade food than chocolate bars.

INGREDIENTS
MAKES ABOUT 16 BARS

300g (11oz) butter, at room temperature, plus extra for greasing
125g (4 ½oz) caster sugar
1 egg
175g (6oz) plain flour
175g (6oz) soft brown sugar
2 tbsp golden syrup
½ tsp fresh lemon juice
400g (14oz) roasted unsalted skinless peanuts

METHOD

Preheat the oven to 180°C (350°F), Gas mark 4, lightly grease a 18 x 27cm (7 x 11in) baking tin and then line the base and sides with parchment paper that is hanging over the sides.

Using an electric beater, cream 100g (4oz) of the butter with the caster sugar in a bowl until light and fluffy. Add the egg and beat well to combine. Sift the flour into a separate bowl and then fold into the butter mixture using a large metal spoon until just combined. Press into the lined tin and bake for 15 minutes or until firm and very lightly browned. Leave to cool for 10 minutes.

Place the remaining butter in a heavy-based pan with the brown sugar, golden syrup and lemon juice.

Cook over low heat for a couple of minutes until the sugar has dissolved, stirring continuously. Increase the heat slightly and simmer for another 5 minutes, stirring.

Remove the toffee from the heat and stir in the peanuts. Using two spoons, spread evenly over the shortbread base, being very careful as the mixture is extremely hot. Return to the oven for another 5 minutes to help the toffee to set. Remove from the oven and leave to cool in tin for 15 minutes, then turn out and cut into squares or small bars. To serve, arrange on plates or wrap in greaseproof paper to take on picnics or in packed lunches.

OATS AND CHOCOLATE COOKIES

These cookies are great to get kids into the kitchen. That is where I started, doing flapjacks, cookies and butterfly cakes with my mother. This gets children cooking something they will eat and that they can take to school. And you will know what is in it. These may not be the healthiest option, but everyone needs some sugar. They make a delicious accompaniment to tea or coffee. Make them on a rainy afternoon and eat them while still warm from the oven. If there are any left, they can be stored in an airtight tin for up to one week. We serve them in our bedrooms for overnight guests.

INGREDIENTS
MAKES 18-20

50g (2oz) caster sugar
100g (4oz) soft brown sugar
250g (9oz) butter, at room temperature
200g (7oz) self-raising flour
100g (4oz) plain or milk chocolate drops
175g (6oz) porridge oats
100g (4oz) chopped nuts, such as walnuts or almonds or use a mixture

METHOD

Preheat oven to 180°C (350°F), Gas mark 4. Cream together both sugars and the butter in a large bowl until light and fluffy. Beat in the flour and then fold in the chocolate drops, porridge oats and nuts. Mix well to combine.

Using your hands, form the mixture into 18-20 small balls, then flattened slightly with a fork. Place them on baking sheets lined with parchment paper, leaving enough room for the cookies to spread out.

Bake in the oven for 15-20 minutes. When they are done, remove from the oven and allow to settle and harden for a minute or two, then transfer to a wire rack with a fish slice and leave cool completely. Store in an airtight container and serve on plates as required.

SWEET SCONES

This is my basic scone recipe; the scones cook in 15 minutes. You can also turn the dough into one large loaf. Cut a deep cross in the centre and bake in the preheated oven for 20 minutes, then reduce the heat to 200°C (400°F), Gas mark 6 and continue to cook for another 20 minutes until the base sounds hollow when tapped.

INGREDIENTS

MAKES 10

450g (1lb) plain flour, plus extra for dusting
1 tsp salt
1 tsp bicarbonate of soda or baking powder
1 tsp caster sugar
25g (1oz) butter
250ml (9fl oz) buttermilk
1 egg, beaten
whipped cream and strawberry jam, to serve (optional)

METHOD

Sift the flour into a bowl with the salt and bicarbonate of soda or baking powder. Stir in the sugar and then, using your fingertips, rub in the butter until the mixture resembles fine breadcrumbs. Make a well in the centre and pour in the buttermilk and beaten egg. Using a tablespoon, gently and quickly stir the liquid into the flour. It should be soft but not sticky. Lightly flour the work surface. Turn the dough out onto it and pat into a circle about 2.5cm (1in) thick. Cut into triangles with a sharp knife or stamp out 5cm (2in) rounds with a cutter.

Arrange the scones on a non-stick baking sheet and bake for 15 minutes until well risen and golden brown. Leave to cool for at least 10 minutes on a wire rack, then serve with the cream and jam, if liked.

VARIATIONS

NUTTY

Use half granary malted flour and half plain flour, then add 1–2 tablespoons finely chopped nuts or toasted sesame seeds or pinhead oatmeal to the mix before adding the buttermilk.

CHEDDAR

Mix 25g (1oz) grated mature Cheddar in with the buttermilk. Brush the finished scones with melted butter and sprinkle with another 75g (3 oz) grated mature Cheddar before baking. Mix 1 teaspoon wholegrain mustard into 25g (1oz) butter and use to spread on the split baked scones before topping with hand-carved cooked ham to serve.

FRUIT

Add 50g (2oz) sultanas or raisins or dried pitted cherries when stirring the sugar into the dry ingredients, then finish as described above.

APPLE AND GINGER CAKE

Hot or cold, this cake is a knockout! You can make it several hours in advance and leave it to cool. This gives the juices time to be well absorbed into the apples and allows the toffee to set slightly. Otherwise it will keep for five to six days in an airtight container.

INGREDIENTS
SERVES 4-6

FOR THE TOPPING:

75g (3oz) butter
125g (4 ½oz) soft brown sugar
4 Bramley apples

FOR THE GINGERBREAD:

100g (4oz) butter
175g (6oz) plain flour
½ tsp baking soda
1 tbsp ground cinnamon
2 tsp ground ginger
½ tsp ground nutmeg
pinch of ground cloves
2 eggs, beaten
175g (6oz) soft brown sugar
125g (4 ½oz) black treacle
150ml (¼ pint) milk
whipped cream, to serve

METHOD

Preheat the oven to 180°C (350°F), Gas mark 4. Butter a 23cm (9 in) non-stick spring-form cake tin and line the base with parchment paper. To make the topping, melt the butter and sugar together in a small pan over a medium-low heat until bubbling, then continue to cook for a few minutes, until creamy and toffee coloured, stirring occasionally.

Pour into the cake tin, tipping the tin to spread the toffee evenly over the base. Peel the apples, then cut in half and cut out their cores. Arrange the apples, cut side down on top of the toffee mixture, with the stalk ends pointing in towards the centre.

To make the gingerbread, melt the butter in a small pan or in the microwave and then set aside to cool slightly. Sift the flour into a large bowl with the baking soda, cinnamon, ginger, nutmeg and cloves. In a separate bowl, place the reserved melted butter with the beaten eggs, sugar, treacle and milk.

Make a well in the centre of the flour mixture and then gradually add the liquid, mixing gently to make a smooth batter. Pour into the tin over the apples. Bake for about 45-55 minutes or until a toothpick or skewer pushed into the middle of the cake comes out barely moist.

Transfer to a wire rack and leave the pudding to cool for a few minutes, then run a knife around the edge of the cake to make sure it is not sticking. Put on some oven gloves and place a large plate on top of the cake tin, turn the whole thing over as quickly as possible. To serve, cut into slices and arrange on plates while still warm. Add a dollop of cream to each slice.

Rathmines Branch Tel: 4973539
Brainse Ráth Maonas Fón: 4973539

WHITE CHOCOLATE CUP CAKES

These cup cakes originated in the USA and are very easy to make. You'll find them a massive hit with children and adults alike. If your tin is not non-stick simply line with deep paper cases.

INGREDIENTS
MAKES 12

250g (9oz) butter, at room temperature, plus extra for greasing
175g (6oz) self-raising flour, sifted
250g (9oz) caster sugar
4 eggs
1 tsp vanilla extract
50g (2oz) plain flour, sifted
175ml (6fl oz) milk
12 mini chocolate Easter eggs
2 teaspoons of multi-coloured sprinkles

FOR THE WHITE CHOCOLATE ICING:

400g (14oz) icing sugar
100g (4oz) white chocolate, broken into pieces
few drops vanilla extract
finely grated rind of 1 orange

METHOD

Preheat oven to 180°C (350°F), Gas mark 4. Grease a 12-hole non-stick muffin tin. Place the butter and sugar in a bowl and beat until pale and creamy. Add a little of the flour, then slowly add eggs and vanilla extract, mixing well to combine.

Slowly add the remaining self raising and the plain flour to the butter and sugar mixture with the milk and beat until just smooth. Divide the mixture between the muffin holes and bake for 20 minutes until well risen and golden brown. Remove from the oven and leave to sit for 10 minutes in the tin. Turn the cup cakes out on to a wire rack to cool completely.

Meanwhile, make the icing. Mix the icing sugar in a bowl with one tablespoon of water to make a thick paste. Melt the white chocolate in the microwave in a heatproof bowl or set over a pan of simmering water. Leave to cool a little, then stir in the icing sugar paste and add the vanilla extract and orange rind, beating with a wooden spoon until smooth.

Cover the cooled cup cakes with the white chocolate icing and top each one with a mini chocolate egg and a dusting of sprinkles, if liked. To serve, arrange on a tiered cake stand or on a plate in a pyramid.

MAIREAD'S SPONGE CAKE

This recipe was given to me by my good friend Mairead Lavery who looks after my column at the Farmer's Journal. It is what she whips up when visitors are coming in the door and she has nothing nice in the press. It can be on the table in 20 minutes. It is delicious with any fresh fruit such as raspberries, strawberries or even a drained can of peach slices; whatever you have to hand really!

INGREDIENTS
SERVES 6

5 eggs, at room temperature
150g (5oz) caster sugar
175g (6oz) self raising flour, sifted
drop of vanilla essence (optional)
knob of butter, for greasing
120ml (4fl oz) cream
2-3 tbsp strawberry, raspberry or apricot
jam icing sugar, to dust

METHOD

Preheat the oven to 180°C (350°F), Gas mark 4. Place the eggs and sugar in a good sized bowl and using either a hand or electric whisk, beat the mixture until it fills over half the bowl and has the consistency of lightly whipped cream.

Using a dessertspoon gently fold in the sifted flour and continue folding until all the flour is fully absorbed, then beat in the vanilla essence. Divide the mixture between 2 x 20cm (8in) sponge cake tins, which have been lightly greased with butter. Cook for 10-12 minutes. When the cake is cooked when it comes slightly away from the tin. Turn out on to wire racks and leave to cool completely.

To serve, whip the cream in a bowl until soft peaks form. Spread the jam on one side of the sponge almost but not quite to the edge and then cover with the cream. Carefully place the other sponge on top to cover the filling completely. Add a light dusting of icing sugar and place on a cake stand, then cut into slices to serve.

MULTISEED BREAD

This is the first thing we make every morning at the restaurant so that guests who have stayed overnight wake up to the smell wafting around the house. It is delicious sprinkled with a couple of tablespoons of sesame seeds or sunflower seeds before baking. If you don't have any buttermilk in the house to use, sour ordinary milk with the juice of a lemon.

INGREDIENTS
MAKES 2 LOAVES

rapeseed or sunflower oil, for greasing
450g (1lb) plain flour, plus extra for dusting
450g (1lb) coarse wholemeal flour
2 tsp baking soda
2 tsp salt
100g (4oz) wheat bran
100g (4oz) mixed seeds, such as linseed, sunflower, sesame seeds and poppy seeds
50g (2oz) butter plus extra to serve
2 tbsp golden syrup
2 tbsp Demerara sugar
1 litre (1 3/4 pints) buttermilk, plus a little extra if necessary

METHOD

Preheat the oven to 180°C (350°F), Gas mark 4 and lightly oil 2 x 1.2 litre (2 pint) loaf tins. Sift the flours, baking soda and salt into a large bowl. Tip in the bran left in the sieve and stir in with the wheat bran with all but one tablespoon of the seeds (reserve them for the top). Rub in the butter with your fingertips until evenly dispersed.

Make a well in the centre of the dry ingredients and add the golden syrup, brown sugar and buttermilk. Using a large spoon, mix gently and quickly until you have achieved a nice fairly wet dropping consistency being careful of any pockets of flour.

Divide the mixture evenly between the prepared loaf tins, spreading it evenly and smoothing the tops with the back of a spoon. Sprinkle over the reserved tablespoon of the seeds.

Bake for 2 hours until well risen and cracked on the top and when a skewer comes out clean when inserted in the centre.

To check the loaves are properly cooked, tip each one out of the tin and tap the base. It should sound hollow. Leave to cool in the tins for about 5 minutes before tipping out on to a wire rack and leave to cool completely. To serve, place the brown wheaten bread on a bread board and cut into slices at the table. Hand around with a separate pot of butter for spreading.

CHEDDAR AND SPRING ONION WHITE SODA BREAD

There is nothing like the smell of baking bread. In the restaurant, we bake every evening before we open, so it is always fresh. It doesn't really keep, so this bread is always best eaten the day it is made. To check that this loaf is properly cooked, tap the base. It should sound hollow. If it doesn't return it to the oven for another 5 minutes. If you don't have any buttermilk in the house to use, sour ordinary milk with the juice of a lemon. Experiment with other flavourings such as crispy pieces of smoked bacon or finely chopped sun-dried tomatoes.

INGREDIENTS
MAKES 1 LOAF

450g (1lb) plain flour, plus extra for dusting
1 tsp bicarbonate of soda
1 tsp salt
100g (4oz) strong Cheddar cheese, grated
4 spring onions, finely chopped
350ml (12fl oz) buttermilk, plus a little extra if necessary

METHOD

Preheat the oven to 230°C (450°F), Gas mark 8. Sift the flours, bicarbonate of soda and salt into a bowl.

Make a well in the centre of the dry ingredients and stir in the Cheddar and spring onions, then add the buttermilk. Using a large spoon, mix gently and quickly until you have achieved a nice soft dough. Add a little bit more buttermilk if necessary until the dough binds together without being sloppy.

Knead the dough very lightly on a lightly floured surface and then shape into a round that is roughly 15cm (6in). Place on a non-stick baking sheet and cut a deep cross in the top.

Bake for 15 minutes, then reduce the temperature to 200°C (400°F), Gas mark 6 and bake for another 20-25 minutes or until the loaf is evenly golden and crusty. It should sound hollow when tapped on the bottom.

Transfer the cooked soda bread to a wire rack and leave to cool for about 20 minutes. This bread is best eaten while it is still warm. To serve, place the soda bread on a breadboard and cut into slices at the table.

BROWN SODA BREAD

Use about three-quarters plain flour to one quarter coarse stoneground wholemeal and add two tablespoons of pinhead oatmeal to the mix before adding the buttermilk.

TOMATO AND PARMESAN TWISTER BREAD ROLLS

These bread rolls are really very easy to make, and baking is coming back big time. We serve them at the beginning of meals in the restaurant. Young people, in particular, love them. Of course, you can vary the toppings, but be careful to go light on them or the fillings may burn while they are cooking.

INGREDIENTS
MAKES 20 ROLLS

1 tbsp olive oil, plus extra for greasing
350g (12oz) strong plain bread flour, plus extra for dusting
1 tsp salt
2 tsp fast action dried yeast (7g sachet)
300ml (½ pint) tepid water
1 egg beaten with 1 tbsp milk

FOR THE FILLING:

200g (7oz) tomato sauce (shop-bought or homemade. See recipie p.96)
125g (4 ½oz) basil pesto (see recipie p.126)
75g (3oz) freshly grated Parmesan

METHOD

Preheat the oven to 200°C (400°F), Gas mark 6. Lightly oil 2 x 12 hole muffin tins. Sieve the flour into a large bowl with the salt and stir in the yeast. Make a well in the centre and pour in the tablespoon of oil and the tepid water. Mix to a smooth dough.

Turn the dough out on to a lightly floured surface and knead to 5-10 minutes, pushing and stretching until smooth and elastic. Alternatively use a food mixer with the dough hook attached and set on a low speed-it saves quite a bit of elbow grease. Place in a large, lightly oiled bowl. Cover with a clean cloth and leave in a warm place for 1 hour until it has doubled in size.

Knock the risen dough back punching it lightly to knock out large air bubbles and knead briefly on a lightly floured surface. Roll out the dough into a large rectangular shape (approximately 55cm (22in) long & 35cm (14in) wide) with a rolling pin. Using a palette knife, spread over the tomato sauce and then spread the pesto on top. Sprinkle over the Parmesan and then gently roll the dough into a long Swiss roll shape. This means that the dough was on the work surface with short ends on either side, then you pick up long end closest to you and roll away from you, don't worry if it sticks a little, just gently coax it up a bit at a time with floured fingers until it reaches the other side and then press seam together to stick.

Cut the flavoured dough into 4cm (1 ½in) thick slices and place one into each muffin hole, one of the cut sides down. Brush the tops lightly with egg wash and leave rise in a warm place for another 10 minutes or until doubled in size. Bake the twister bread rolls for 20-25 minutes; swapping the tins around on shelves half way through until cooked through and golden brown. Leave for a couple of minutes in the tin before Loosen the bread rolls from the muffin tins with a knife and slide out on to a wire rack. Serve warm or leave to cool completely before serving.

176

The Ultimate Christmas

STARTERS PLATTER

When you have a crowd in the house at Christmas what could be nicer than a platter of nibbles with something for everyone. All recipes can be prepared in advance leaving very little to do last minute except enjoy your guests!

HOMEMADE SAUSAGE ROLLS WITH SESAME SEEDS

These sausage rolls can be frozen uncooked for up to one month. Layer up between sheets of paper in a plastic rigid container and secure with a lid before freezing. Increase the cooking time by about 10 minutes if cooking straight from frozen

INGREDIENTS

MAKES ABOUT 40

25g (1oz) butter, plus extra for greasing
2 tbsp finely diced onion
3 eggs
450g (1lb) sausage meat (good quality)
2 tbsp sweet chilli sauce
1 tbsp chopped fresh basil
1 tbsp cream
375g packet (8oz) ready-rolled puff pastry, thawed if frozen
2 tbsp sesame seeds
butter, for greasing
salt and freshly ground black pepper

METHOD

Preheat the oven to 220°C (425°F), Gas mark 7. Melt the butter in a frying pan and sauté the onion for about 5 minutes until softened but not coloured. Remove from the heat and leave to cool.

Break two of the eggs into a food processor or liquidiser and add the sausage meat, sweet chilli sauce, basil and cream. Blend for 2 minutes until smooth, then scrape out into a bowl with a spatula and stir in the cooked onions. Season to taste and place mixture in piping bag with 2.5cm (1in) plain nozzle.

Beat the remaining egg in a small bowl with a pinch of salt and set aside for glazing. Place the puff pastry on a lightly floured surface and cut into four strips, each measuring 25cm (10in) x 7.5cm (3in). Pipe the sausage meat mixture down the centre of each pastry strip and brush along one long edge with a little egg of the beaten egg. Roll up to enclose and press down the edges firmly to seal.

Brush the sausage rolls with the beaten egg and sprinkle lightly with the sesame seeds. Cut into 2.5cm (1in) lengths and arrange on lightly buttered large baking sheets. Bake for 15 minutes or until crisp and golden.

To serve, arrange the sausage rolls on a warmed serving platter and hand around with napkins.

STICKY BEEF SKEWERS

It is important to soak the bamboo skewers you need for this recipe for at least half an hour before using them, otherwise they'll burn under the grill. However, if you do forget – all's not lost, simply cook them on a griddle pan, problem solved! To make your own garlic and chive mayonnaise, simply stir two crushed garlic cloves and two tablespoons snipped fresh chives into 150ml (¼ pint) of mayonnaise.

INGREDIENTS
MAKES ABOUT 20

2 garlic cloves, crushed
3 tbsp clear honey
1 tbsp Worcestershire sauce
1 tbsp dark soy sauce
1 tbsp balsamic vinegar
1 tsp wholegrain mustard
900g (2lb) sirloin steak, trimmed and cut into thin strips
garlic and chive mayonnaise, to serve

METHOD

Place the garlic in a shallow non-metallic dish and add the honey, Worcestershire sauce, soy sauce, balsamic vinegar and mustard. Mix until well combined. Thread the sirloin strips on to 20 x (10cm) 4in soaked bamboo skewers and add the marinade, turning to coat. Cover with clingfilm and chill for at least 6 hours or up to 24 hours in fridge.

Preheat the grill. Drain the beef skewers, reserving any remaining marinade and arrange on a grill rack. Cook for 8-10 minutes, turning once and brushing regularly with the remaining marinade until cooked through and well caramelised. To serve, arrange the sticky beef skewers on a large warmed serving platter around a bowl of garlic and chive mayonnaise for dipping.

SMOKED SALMON AND CREAM CHEESE ON RITZ CRACKERS

These canapés literally take minutes to make and the smoked salmon mixture can be made up to one week in advance and kept covered with clingfilm in the fridge. The crackers can be chosen according to personal preference and are a useful standby to keep in the cupboard. Just don't be tempted to pipe the smoked salmon mixture on the crackers too soon or they will go soggy.

INGREDIENTS
MAKES ABOUT 20

300g (11oz) full fat cream cheese
225g (8oz) Irish smoked salmon, finely chopped
1 tbsp sweet chilli sauce
1 tsp chopped fresh parsley
1 tsp fresh lemon juice
150g packet Ritz or mini Tuc crackers
salt and freshly ground black pepper
chopped fresh flat-leaf parsley, to garnish

METHOD

Place the cream cheese in a food processor with the smoked salmon, sweet chilli sauce, parsley and lemon juice. Blitz until smooth and then season to taste. Spoon into a piping bag fitted with a 1cm (½in) fluted nozzle and place in fridge for at least 30 minutes and up to 24 hours to firm up.

To serve, pipe the smoked salmon cream cheese on to the crackers and arrange on a large serving platter. Garnish with a light sprinkling of the parsley.

CHICKEN DIPPERS

These chicken dippers can be prepared the day before they are needed and just popped into the oven when you are ready for them. Kids just love them and they taste so much nicer than shop-bought nuggets. They can also be cooked in a deep-fat fryer but obviously it's much healthier to bake them in the oven. Serve them with your favourite sauce for dipping such as sweet chilli sauce, tomato ketchup or a yoghurt & carrot raita.

INGREDIENTS
MAKES ABOUT 20

150g (5oz) fresh white breadcrumbs
1 tbsp sesame seeds
1 tbsp chopped fresh flat-leaf parsley
2 tbsp medium curry powder
2 tbsp plain flour
2 eggs, beaten
450g (1oz) skinless chicken breast fillets
olive oil, for greasing
yoghurt & carrot raita, to serve (optional)

METHOD

Preheat the oven to 180°C (350°F), Gas mark 4. Place the breadcrumbs in a food processor or liquidiser with the sesame seeds, parsley and curry powder. Blend for 2 minutes until well combined and then tip into a shallow dish.

Place the flour on a flat plate and season to taste. Place the eggs in a shallow dish. Cut the chicken fillets into about 20 even-sized strips and then toss each one into seasoned flour, shaking off any excess.

Dip the coated chicken strips into the beaten egg and then coat in the breadcrumbs. Arrange on an oiled large baking sheet, well spaced apart. Bake for 10 minutes or until cooked through and until golden brown. To serve, arrange the chicken dippers on a warmed serving platter with a bowl yoghurt and carrot raita.

ROAST TURKEY WITH SAGE, APRICOT AND PINE NUT STUFFING

If you want to be sure that your turkey is cooked invest in a meat thermometer and push it into the thickest part of one of the thighs. This will then clearly show you when the turkey is cooked, leaving no doubt in your mind. Ask your butcher for the giblets with your turkey as they make excellent stock. I always soak mine in cold water overnight to remove any impurities. Place them in a pan with a chopped carrot and onion, six whole peppercorns, two bay leaves and a sprig to thyme. Pour in 2 pints (1.2 litres) of water and bring to the boil, then reduce the heat and simmer for 45 minutes. Strain and use as required.

INGREDIENTS
SERVES 10-12)

6kg (12lb) oven-ready turkey, at room temperature (preferably free-range)
100g (4oz) butter, at room temperature
4 rindless streaky bacon rashers
150g (5oz) ready-to-eat pitted prunes
450g (1oz) cocktail sausages
1 tbsp plain flour
3 tbsp ruby red port or red wine
600ml (1 pint) turkey or chicken stock (see introduction)

FOR THE SAGE, ONION AND PINE NUT STUFFING:

50g (2oz) pine nuts
75g (3oz) butter
1 large onion, diced
175g (6oz) fresh white breadcrumbs
1 tbsp chopped fresh parsley
1 tsp chopped fresh sage

4 ready-to-eat dried apricots, finely chopped
salt and freshly ground black pepper
Crispy roast potatoes with thyme and garlic (page 198), Roast root vegetables with honey and parsley and Brussels sprout, red onion and bacon crumble (page 200) small bunch fresh herbs, to garnish (to include parsley, sage and bay leaves)

METHOD

Preheat the oven to 190°C (375°F), Gas mark 5. To make the stuffing, heat a frying pan. Add the pine nuts and cook until toasted, tossing occasionally to prevent them from catching. Tip into a bowl. Melt the butter in the same pan and add the onion, then cook for a few minutes until softened but not coloured. Place the breadcrumbs in a bowl and tip in the toasted pine nuts, onion and

butter mixture, parsley, sage and apricots. Mix well to combine and season to taste. To stuff the turkey, start at the neck end where you'll find a flap of loose skin: gently loosen this away from the breast and you'll be able to make a triangular pocket. Pack in the stuffing inside as far as you can go and make a neat round shape on the outside, then tuck the neck flap under the turkey's and secure it with a small skewer.

Cut bacon into small strips and use to wrap prunes. Arrange on a plate with the cocktail sausages, cover with clingfilm and chill until needed. Smear the skin of the turkey all over with some of the butter and season generously. Turn the turkey breast-side up and tie the top of the drumsticks with string. Weigh the turkey to calculate the required cooking time, allowing 20 minutes per 450g (1lb) plus 20 minutes extra – this size turkey should take about 4 hours and 20 minutes.

Lay a large sheet of foil lengthways over a large roasting tin, leaving enough at each end to wrap over the turkey, then lightly butter the foil. Repeat this exercise with another sheet of foil, this time across the tin. Lightly butter once again. Place the stuffed turkey breast-side up in the centre of the foil, then wrap loosely to enclose, allowing air to circulate around the turkey.

Place in the oven and cook according to your calculated cooking time, carefully unwrapping and basting every 40 minutes. For the final hour, fold back and remove the foil, keeping the ends of the drumsticks still covered in foil to prevent them from burning; baste well and return to the oven.

Add the bacon wrapped prunes and cocktail sausages to the turkey for the last 30 minutes and allow to finish cooking. The turkey should be a rich, dark brown colour. To be sure its cooked, insert a fine skewer into the thickest part of the thigh: the juices should run clear, but if they are still pink, return the turkey to the oven and check again every 15 minutes until you are happy that the turkey is cooked right the way through.

Remove from the oven and transfer to a serving platter, surround with the bacon wrapped prunes and cocktail sausages. Cover with foil and leave to rest in a warm place for 10 minutes or up to 30 minutes is fine.

Place the roasting tin directly on the hob over a gentle heat and skim any excess fat from the cooking juices. Stir the flour into the tin's residue. Cook on the hob for a minute or two, stirring until golden. Pour in the port or red wine, stirring to combine, then gradually add the stock, stirring until smooth after each addition. Bring to the boil and let it bubble for about 10 minutes until reduced and thickened, stirring occasionally. Season to taste.

To serve, garnish the turkey with the bunch of herbs in the neck cavity and bring to the table. Carve into slices and arrange on warmed serving plates with some of the gravy, the roast potatoes, vegetables and all of the trimmings.

ROAST GOOSE WITH APPLE AND CRANBERRY STUFFING

INGREDIENTS
SERVES 8

6kg (12lb) oven-ready goose
2 eating apples, peeled, cored and cut into wedges
100g (4oz) fresh cranberries
24 asparagus spears, peeled
1 tsp salt
2 tbsp redcurrant jelly
1 tbsp ruby red port or red wine
finely grated rind of 1 orange

FOR THE APPLE AND CRANBERRY STUFFING:

2 tbsp olive oil
2 eating apples, peeled, cored and cut into thin slices
1 tbsp chopped fresh thyme
350g (12oz) sausage meat (good quality)
75g (3oz) fresh white breadcrumbs
100g (4oz) dried cranberries
100g (4oz) walnut halves, chopped
salt and freshly ground black pepper
Crispy roast potatoes with thyme and garlic (page 00), Roast root vegetables with honey and parsley and Brussels sprout, red onion and bacon crumble (page 00)
small bunch fresh thyme sprigs, to garnish

METHOD

To make the stuffing, heat the oil in a large frying pan. Add the apples and sauté for 3-4 minutes until softened and golden. Transfer to a bowl and leave to cool. Add the thyme, sausage meat, breadcrumbs, cranberries and walnuts, stirring gently until evenly mixed. Season to taste.

Preheat oven to 200°C (400°F), Gas mark 6. Place the goose on a rack set over a roasting tin. Pour over a full kettle of boiling water, then drain off the water from the roasting tin. To stuff the goose, start at the neck end where you'll find a flap of loose skin: gently loosen this away from the breast and you'll be able to make a triangular pocket. Pack in two-thirds of the stuffing inside as far as you can go and make a neat round shape on the outside, then tuck the neck flap under the goose and secure it with a small skewer. Rub all over with salt.

Press the remaining stuffing into the base of 450g (1lb) loaf tin and set aside. Weigh the goose and calculate the cooking time, allowing 15 minutes per 450g (1lb) plus 15 minutes – this goose should take about 3 ½ hours. Place in the oven to roast, draining off excess fat every 30 minutes or so and after 1 hour reduce the oven temperature to 180°C (350°F), Gas mark 4. Continue to cook, still draining the fat off every half an hour.

Remove the goose from the oven 30 minutes before the end of the cooking time. Drain off all but two tablespoons of the fat and add the apple wedges, cranberries and asparagus, tossing to coat. Warm the redcurrant jelly in a small pan or in the microwave and stir in the port or wine with the orange rind, then brush over the goose. Return the goose to the oven with the reserved tin of extra stuffing and cook for the final 30 minutes until completely tender. Transfer the goose to a serving platter and cover with foil, then leave to rest for 10 minutes. Place the cranberry, apple and asparagus mixture into a warmed serving bowl and keep warm.

To serve, garnish with roast goose with the thyme and bring to the table. Turn the tin of extra stuffing on to a warmed serving plate. Carve into slices and arrange on warmed serving plates, discarding any excess fat with some of the stuffing, roasted cranberries, apples and asparagus, the roast potatoes and vegetables.

IRISH WHISKEY AND MAPLE GLAZED HAM

A traditional ham is the perfect choice if you've got hoards of visitors to feed so it's especially good to have over the festive period. Any leftovers from this ham or your turkey can be used in countless other dishes, such as in a creamy filling for vol-au-vents, in risottos or just the ham is excellent for a spaghetti carbonara, so there's no waste – even the bone will make a wonderful stock.

INGREDIENTS
SERVES 10-12

5.25kg (11lb) leg of gammon (on the bone)
4 celery sticks, roughly chopped
2 onions, sliced
1 bunch fresh thyme
1 tbsp black peppercorns
200ml (7fl oz) Irish whiskey
200ml (7fl oz) maple syrup
3 tsp ground allspice
1 tsp whole cloves

METHOD

Although gammon is less salty nowadays, soaking is still a good idea. Place the gammon in a large pan and cover with cold water. Leave to soak for at least 6 hours or overnight is best, then drain.

Weigh the gammon joint and calculate the cooking time, allowing 20 minutes per 450g (1lb) plus 20 minutes – this joint should take about 4 hours. Place in a large pan and cover with water and bring to the boil, skimming off any scum. Add the celery, onions, thyme and peppercorns and return to the boil, then cover, reduce the heat and simmer until completely tender, occasionally skimming off any scum that rises to the top. If you are not sure about whether the gammon is properly cooked check the bone end – it should come away freely from the gammon joint. Drain and leave until cool enough to handle.

Preheat the oven to 180°C (350°F), Gas mark 4. Carefully peel away the skin, leaving the layer of white fat intact. Using a sharp knife, score the fat diagonally to make a diamond pattern, being careful not to cut into the meat. Place the whiskey in a pan with the maple syrup and ground allspice. Bring to the boil and simmer for about 10 minutes until slightly thickened. Stud the ham with the cloves and place in a large roasting tin with a little water to prevent the bottom from catching and burning. Brush the syrup all over the ham. Cook for 1 hour, basting every 15 minutes to ensure an even glaze. Remove the cooked ham from the oven, transfer to a serving platter and leave to rest for 15 minutes.

Carve slices from one side of the ham, cutting diagonally to achieve an even thickness. When you reach the bone, insert the knife at a flatter angle and slice across the top of the bone. Turn over the leg to carve slices from the other sides, arrange on warmed plates to serve.

BRUSSELS SPROUT, RED ONION AND BACON CRUMBLE

If you are not a fan of Brussels sprouts try using thickly sliced leeks with broccoli or cauliflower instead. This will also make a good vegetarian option for Christmas lunch if you leave out the bacon.

INGREDIENTS
SERVES 8-10

675g (1 ½oz) Brussels sprouts, trimmed
and cut in half
knob of butter
1 large red onion, thinly sliced
2 cooked slices smoked bacon, diced
200ml (7fl oz) cream
50ml (2fl oz) milk
good pinch of freshly grated nutmeg
50g (2oz) fresh white breadcrumbs
25g (1oz) shelled walnuts, chopped
1 tsp chopped fresh flat-leaf parsley
salt and freshly ground black pepper

METHOD

Preheat oven to 190°C (375°F), Gas mark 5. Half fill a pan with water and bring to the boil. Add the Brussels sprouts and simmer for 4-5 minutes until just tender but not soggy. Drain and refresh under running cold water.

Butter a baking dish and tip in the blanched Brussels sprouts. Scatter over the red onion and bacon. Mix the cream with the milk and nutmeg in a jug and season to taste, then pour over the sprouts. Sprinkle the breadcrumbs on top and place in oven for 20-25 minutes until bubbling and golden brown. To serve, place piping hot directly on the table and allow guests to help themselves.

CRISPY ROAST POTATOES WITH THYME AND GARLIC

This recipe will give you really crunchy roast potatoes with fluffy middles. Choose a floury variety of potato and try to make sure that they are all similar in size. Cook them in the vegetable oil or better still use some fat that is leftover from a roast. It really does make the world of difference and as all fats freeze very well there's no excuse not to have some, especially for special occasions like Christmas day. If you want to cook them and the Roasted root vegetables with honey and parsley (See recipie p.194) for the same meal, just put these on the top shelf of the oven the vegetables in the bottom, tossing the vegetables occasionally to prevent them from catching and burning. To ensure really crispy roast potatoes drain off any excess fat about 20 minutes before the end of the cooking time.

INGREDIENTS
SERVES 10-12

1.5kg (3lb) potatoes, halved
about 100ml (3 ½fl oz) sunflower oil,
or dripping, goose or duck fat (see
introduction.)
2 tsp fresh thyme leaves
6 garlic cloves, not peeled
coarse sea salt

METHOD

Preheat the oven to 220°C (425°F), Gas mark 7. Place the potatoes in a pan of cold salted water and bring to the boil. Reduce the heat and simmer for 8-10 minutes until the outsides have just softened. Drain and return to the pan for a minute or two to dry out.

Meanwhile, preheat a roasting tin with a 1cm (½in) depth of oil, dripping, duck or goose fat for a few minutes until just smoking. Roughly prod the outside of the potatoes with a fork and toss them with thyme and garlic. Carefully tip them into the hot oil, basting the tops. Roast for about 45 minutes to 1 hour, turning occasionally, until crisp and golden.

To Serve, transfer the roast potatoes with a slotted spoon into a warmed serving bowl and season with the sea salt and place them directly on the table – eat immediately – they don't hang around!

ROASTED ROOT VEGETABLES WITH HONEY AND PARSLEY

Roasting is a great way to cook root vegetables as they're robust enough to cope with the intense heat, and the honey helps draw out the most wonderful flavours. This recipe also makes life much easier on Christmas day as all the preparation can be done well in advance so there's really nothing to them. Just make sure that all your vegetables are roughly the same size to ensure even cooking. Try using any combination of root vegetables you fancy. However, it's probably worth remembering that beetroot will stain all other root vegetables, so it's probably best to roast them on their own. Any leftovers can be blitzed with stock for an instant soup.

INGREDIENTS
SERVES 10-12

3 tbsp olive oil
1.5kg (3lb) carrots, trimmed and halved lengthways
1.5kg (3lb) large parsnips, trimmed, quartered and cored
3 tbsp clear honey
1 tsp toasted sesame seeds
3 tbsp chopped fresh flat-leaf parsley
salt and freshly ground black pepper

METHOD

Preheat the oven to 180°C (350°F), Gas mark 4. Place the oil in a large roasting tin and add the carrots and parsnips, tossing until well coated. Season generously. Roast for 30 minutes, then drizzle over the honey and toss to coat evenly. Roast for another 10 minutes or until the vegetables are completely tender and lightly charred. Sprinkle over the sesame seeds and parsley and toss gently until evenly coated.

To serve, tip the roasted root vegetables into a serving dish and place directly on the table so that people can help themselves.

AUNTIE MAUREEN'S PLUM PUDDING WITH BRANDY BUTTER

It is hard to believe that Christmas is almost upon us, and nothing beats the flavour of homemade Christmas pudding, so start stirring now. It is very important to get good quality fruit. Aunt Maureen gets hers from Jim's Kitchen in Portlaoise. The advance preparation now will make things easier at Christmas but, apart from that, the tastes will be so much better if made now. I love plum pudding – hot or cold – with lashings of cream. I always look forward to it. A big thank you to Auntie Maureen.

INGREDIENTS
SERVES 10-12

50g (2oz) plain flour
½ tsp ground mixed spice
½ tsp ground nutmeg
½ tsp ground cloves
175g (6oz) fresh white breadcrumbs
175g (6oz) soft brown sugar
175g (6oz) raisins
50g (2oz) currants
225g (8oz) sultanas
50g (2oz) candied mixed peel
50g (2oz) blanched almonds, chopped
½ apple, peeled, cored and diced
½ small carrot, grated
finely grated rind and juice
of 1 lemon
175g (6oz) butter, melted plus extra for greasing
2 eggs, lightly beaten
300ml (½ pint) stout
brandy sauce and whipped cream, to serve

METHOD

Sift together the flour, mixed spice, nutmeg and cloves. Add the breadcrumbs, sugar, raisins, currants, sultanas, mixed peel, almonds, apple, carrot, lemon rind, lemon juice and melted butter and mix until well combined. Gradually add the beaten eggs, stirring constantly followed by the stout. Mix everything thoroughly and cover with a clean tea towel, then leave in a cool place overnight.

Use the fruit mixture to fill into 2 x 1.2 litre (2 pint) greased pudding bowls. Cover with a double thickness of greaseproof paper and tin foil, then tie tightly under the rim with string. Store in a cool, dry place.

To cook, preheat an oven to 150°C (300°F), Gas mark 2 and stand each pudding basin in a large cake tin three quarters full of boiling water, then cook for

6-8 hours. (or you can steam for 6 hours in the usual way) Cool, re-cover with clean greaseproof paper. Again, store in a cool, dry place.

On Christmas Day, re-cover with greaseproof paper and foil. Steam, in the same manner, for 2-3 hours until completely cooked through and tender. Cut the plum pudding into slices and arrange on plates. Serve with dollops of the brandy sauce and whipped cream to serve.

MULLED FRUIT TRIFLE

This is one dessert that I can clearly remember from my childhood – it probably even enticed me to be a chef. My Mum always made this for special occasions and I just loved helping, especially with the cleaning of the bowls…Frozen bags of fruits of the forest are available in most supermarkets but you can experiment with any selection of frozen berries, or fruit for that matter. I just find them incredibly handy, when the fridge is bursting full with yummy things at Christmas.

INGREDIENTS
SERVES 6-8

150ml (¼ pint) ruby red port
75g (3oz) caster sugar
1 tsp ground mixed spice
500g bag frozen fruits of the forest
200g (7oz) Madeira cake, broken into chunks
300ml (½ pint) cream

FOR THE CUSTARD:

300ml (½ pint) milk
200ml (7fl oz) cream
5 egg yolks
4 tbsp caster sugar
2 tsp cornflour
few drops vanilla extract
chocolate curls, to decorate

METHOD

To make the custard, Place the milk and cream in a heavy-based pan over a gentle heat and cook until it nearly reaches the boil – but don't allow to boil. Meanwhile, place the egg yolks, sugar, cornflour, sugar and vanilla essence in a large bowl and whisk together until pale and thickened.

Remove the milk and cream mixture from the heat and then slowly whisk it into the egg mixture until smooth. Pour back into the pan and place on a gentle heat. Cook, without allowing to boil, until the custard coats the back of a wooden spoon, stirring continuously. Remove from the heat and leave to cool, stirring occasionally to prevent a skin forming on top. Place the ruby red port in a large pan with the sugar and mixed spice and then bring to the boil. Reduce the heat and simmer for 5 minutes until syrupy, stirring occasionally. Stir in the frozen fruits of the forest and set aside

until cooled, stirring occasionally. The fruits should defrost naturally in the hot syrup but still hold their shape. Scatter the Madeira cake over the base of a 1.5 litre (2 ½ pint) glass serving bowl. Spoon over the fruits of the forest mixture and cover with the cooled custard. Whip the cream in a bowl until you have achieved soft peaks and place spoonfuls on top of custard, then gently spread with a palette knife to cover the custard completely. Chill for 1 hour, or you can make this up to 24 hours in advance but finish with the whipped cream just before serving.

To serve, sprinkle the chocolate curls over the trifle and place straight on the table, then spoon into individual serving bowls.

MACNEAN OLD-FASHIONED MINCE PIES

Not surprisingly, my Auntie Maureen is also the champion of this Maguire classic. Before she retired, she was a Domestic Science teacher in Cavan, and I don't believe she ever had a pupil who didn't learn how to make her marvellous mince meat pies. Once you've made it yourself, you'll never buy another jar of the stuff again. Why not make twice the amount of mince meat and put in some sterilised fancy jars, wrap with a red ribbon and give a jar to your friends for a Christmas gift.

INGREDIENTS
MAKES ABOUT 40

FOR THE SWEET PASTRY:
100g (4oz) butter
175g (6oz) plain flour
pinch of salt
50g (2oz) caster sugar
1 egg yolk, plus beaten egg to glaze
½ tbsp cream
½ tsp lemon juice

FOR THE MINCEMEAT:

350g (12oz) eating apples
225g (8oz) butter
225g (8oz) raisins
225g (8oz) sultanas
225g (8oz) currants
100g (4oz) mixed peel
175g (6oz) blanched almonds, chopped
175g (6oz) dark brown sugar
finely grated rind 1 orange
finely grated rind 1 lemon
½ tsp ground nutmeg
1 tsp ground cinnamon
½ tsp ground cloves
½ tsp salt
300ml (½ pint) whiskey
icing sugar, to dust

METHOD

To make the mincemeat, peel, core and finely chop apples. Melt the butter in a small pan or in the microwave. Mix all ingredients together in a large bowl and cover with clean a tea cloth. Leave overnight. Mix well and leave for 2 days for the flavours to develop, then pack into clean, dry jars. Seal and store in a cool, dark place for 3 weeks before use.

Preheat the oven to 180°C (350°F), Gas mark 4. To make the pastry, place the butter, flour, salt and sugar into a food processor and blend for 20 seconds. Add the egg yolk and cream and blend again until the pastry just comes together. Do not over-work or the pastry will be tough. Wrap in clingfilm and chill for 1 hour. Roll out half of pastry thinly on a lightly-floured board. Cut out 40 x 6cm (2 ½in) rounds with a cutter and use to line tartlet tins. Fill with the mincemeat.

Roll out the remainder of pastry and cut 40 x 7cm (3 in) with a cutter to fit the tops. Brush the edges of the mince pies with water and place the larger rounds on top, seal with tips of fingers. Make a small slit in each mince pie. Brush with beaten egg. Bake for 15-16 minutes until cooked through and golden brown. Cool in the tins before lifting out the mince pies. Dust with icing sugar and arrange on a large serving platter to serve.

MACNEAN MINT CHOCOLATE TRUFFLES

These truffles make the perfect end to a special lunch served with Irish coffee. However, they also make wonderful gifts for your friends. Experiment with different flavours and try adding rum, cointreau or whiskey or Baileys Irish cream instead of the crème de menthe liqueur and fresh mint.

INGREDIENTS
MAKES ABOUT 40

250ml (9fl oz) cream
250g (9oz) butter
2 tbsp chopped fresh mint
500g (1lb 2oz) plain chocolate, broken
into squares
2 tbsp crème de menthe liqueur

FOR THE COATING:

225g (8oz) plain chocolate, broken
into squares
cocoa powder, for dusting

METHOD

Place the cream and butter in a pan with the mint and bring to the boil. Reduce the heat and then whisk in the chocolate until smooth and melted. Stir in the crème de menthe liqueur and strain into a sieve set over a bowl. Leave to cool completely, then cover with clingfilm and chill for 2–3 hours until set firm, stirring occasionally to present a skin forming.

When mixture is cold and set, scoop into small balls-you can use a large melon baller for this. Make sure to dip the melon baller in hot water to give the chocolate mixture a better shape. Arrange on a baking sheet lined with parchment paper.

To make the coating, melt the chocolate in a heatproof bowl set over a pan of simmering water or in the microwave. Leave to cool a little, then dip the truffles in melted chocolate and quickly roll in the cocoa powder. Place in fridge to set. To serve, arrange the truffles on a plate to hand around to guests whilst they are enjoying their coffee.

Acknowledgements

I really enjoyed bringing together all the recipies from my weekly feature in the Irish Farmers Journal - it was no easy task, but made so much easier thanks to the fantastic support of the team at the Irish Farmers Journal. I've always found them a joy to work with, and the source of continued inspiration. I'd particularly like to thank Mairead Lavery and David Leydon from the Irish Farmers Journal for their dedication to this cookbook.

This book would never had been published if it wasn't for the loyalty of the Irish Farmers Journal readers; thanks to your continued support, and I look forward to providing you with weekly recipies and tips for the coming years.

To all the food producers in Ireland, with whom I share a passion for quality, homegrown produce - despite tough times, our producers continue to provide us with some of the most wholesome foods in the world; we may be a small country, but we certainly know good food!

I always say you are nothing without a good team behind you; with that in mind, I'd like to thank Orla Broderick, Sharon Aherne-Smith, Jack Caffrey and John Masterson for their weekly input into the recipies and food images that adorn the pages of the Irish Farmers Journal. Orla has been the driving force behind selecting and perfecting the recipies in this cookbook; thanks also to Zara McHugh for typing up the recipies and deciphering my difficult to read handwriting!

A special thanks to Sheila Gallogly, Lee Grace, Ann Marie Coonan and Terry Byrne of Márla.ie for all of their hard work in designing and laying out this cookbook.

A particular big thank you goes to John Hickey, who has been instrumental in helping me drive the business forward.

Finally, as always, I want to thank the two most important women in my life. My mother Vera and my beautiful wife Amelda. Thanks for your continuous support; it has been a busy, but wonderful year.